The BUNCO BOOK

The BUNCO BOOK

By

Walter B. Gibson

CITADEL PRESS • SECAUCUS, NEW JERSEY

Copyright © 1946, 1986 by Litvka R. Gibson

Published by Citadel Press
A division of Lyle Stuart Inc.
120 Enterprise Ave., Secaucus, N.J. 07094
In Canada: Musson Book Company
A division of General Publishing Co. Limited
Don Mills, Ontario

Queries regarding rights and permissions should be
addressed to: Lyle Stuart, 120 Enterprise Avenue,
Secaucus, N.J. 07094

Manufactured in the United States of America

ISBN 0-8065-0990-2

"A Word to the Wise" — or Otherwise

To say that this book carries a timely warning would be an understatement. It covers a problem that is always with us: the desire of certain individuals to gain quick money by fair means or foul — and preferably the latter. How these questionable characters operate and how you can guard yourself against them, are the subjects which the volume treats.

Only a man highly qualified in the psychology of deception could have written such a book and the author, Walter B. Gibson, has had a unique career where subjects bordering upon the mysterious are concerned. Prior to writing the "Bunco Book", he was associated with such famous magicians as Thurston and Houdini in the preparation of books and articles on magic. After Houdini's death, Gibson wrote two volumes on Houdini's methods, compiled from the famous wizard's own personal notes. This work was assigned to Gibson because he was the one writer then able to piece together the important details which the notes contained.

Later, Gibson became associated with Blackstone, who today is recognized as the World's Master Magician. This collaboration has continued steadily through the years. At present Blackstone is supplying Gibson with biographical and technical material for what may well become the most remarkable book ever devoted to the magic art.

In the field of fiction, Gibson's career reads like something he himself imagined. From his study of the shady devices so thoroughly described in the "Bunco Book" he delved into an analysis of criminal methods. To drive home the message that "Crime Does Not Pay" he personalized a champion of law and order in the character of "The Shadow" which appeared in novel-length form in a magazine bearing the same title.

So completely did "The Shadow" stories capture public interest that for fifteen years, Gibson was busy writing more of them, all of his stories appearing under the pen-name of Maxwell Grant. As the original author of these novels, he delivered more that two hundred and seventy-five in the period stated above, at an average of a million words a year. If printed in book form — in which a few were later issued — these novels would fill more than thirty feet of book-shelves.

In setting what was questionably an all-time record in writing the adventures of a single mystery character, Gibson drew constantly upon the type of source material found in such works as his "Bunco Book". As the years passed, this volume, long out of print, gained recognition as the most lucid and most diversified publication in its particular field.

This at least was the impression of the publisher of the present edition, Sidney H. Radner, whose own interest in magic had led him into similar channels. In studying the methods of escape artists, Radner decided to put them into practice after meeting Hardeen, the brother of Houdini. Not only was Radner instructed by Hardeen, but the later supplied him with much of the original Houdini equipment, including the famous Water Torture Cell, the device from which Houdini alone had ever attempted to escape.

Serving in the Army during World War II, Radner not only performed escape feats for his fellow-soldiers but found his knowledge of gambling methods of great importance. Soon he was informing the G I's on the ins and outs of such practices, under official auspices. Later, he was made a secret agent of the Criminal Investigation Division, the Army's F.B.I., for the purpose of investigating crooked gambling in the China – India – Burma theatre of operations. With the conclusion of the War, Radner, as a veteran who had served overseas, was more than aware of the lures that might await the returning service man, where matters of money were concerned. He decided to follow up his experience by producing a publication which would serve as a detour sign against the pitfalls laid by sharpers.

Mutual interest resulted in a meeting between Walter Gibson, author of the "Bunco Book" and Sidney Radner, who had long recognized the practical and permanent value of that publication. The outcome was this new edition of a basic volume which fills a purpose distinctively its own.

The ways of bunco artists are not limited by time or place, but there are flush periods and certain localities that produce a flood of such operators. This Post-War period is such a time and the whole range of the United States is the territory. This book is therefore presented for the protection of the unwary. The methods which it reveals are already known to the leeches who specialize in such devices and therefore can be of no value to them; but if it educates the uninitiated — as it will — there will be less victims and even those will come harder.

The only admonition is that the reader should remember the old proverb of a little learning being a dangerous thing. Don't think that some game is on the level because it seems to reverse a rule that you read in these pages. Crooked rules are the sort that read both ways. So be on guard against new twists.

When strangers ask for sympathy, let them have it; but not on a cash basis. If somebody has a scheme for getting rich, remember that if it worked, he would be using it himself. As for gambling, whether in dimes or dollars, count it up in terms of time that will be lost and you will find that you can't even begin to win.

This is not free advice, the kind that is too cheap to have a value. Having paid for this book, you deserve dividends on your investment. This book tells you how to save your money so you will be a satisfied customer for a further volume on the subject. So don't fall for something phoney in the meanwhile. Wait until you have a chance to read about it and find out what a nice opportunity it was to miss.

CONTENTS

The BUNCO BOOK

The bunco man actually sells a real gold brick.

The Gold Brick Game

*Reviewing and Shedding Light
on the Most Notorious of Swindles*

A LL is not gold that glitters."
Plenty of people have
learned this to their sorrow.
The gold brick swindle is an old
one; but it has duped plenty of
shrewd business men.

The average person thinks that
anyone who will buy a gold brick
must be a real sucker indeed. Such
is not the case. Gold brick swindlers are among the cleverest
workers in the business.

They approach a man and tell
him that they can obtain a gold
brick worth $8000 for half that
price. They always have a story
to go with it; the brick may have
been stolen; it may belong to an
ignorant man who does not know
its value; or it may be the legitimate property of an old miner
who needs money and who is
afraid to sell the brick openly for
fear that he will be questioned

about it, and cannot prove that
it belongs to him.

The Gold Brick Is Real

At any rate, these swindlers actually sell a real gold brick. They
induce their victim to travel to a
neighboring city where he is
shown the brick by the man who
is supposed to own it. He is allowed to test the brick, and he
finds it to be real gold. The brick
is placed in a suitcase and the
sucker departs with it.

Introducing the Phoney Brick

But besides the real gold brick
the gyps have a phoney one, a brass
brick, which is in a duplicate suitcase, heavily weighted to make it
feel the same as the satchel containing the genuine brick.

Before the victim gets home,
these fellows see to it that the suit-
cases are exchanged, and the fraud
is completed. There are various
ways by which this is done. Sometimes the brick is switched before
the sucker leaves the house of the
old man who had the brick. At
any rate, the victim is often taken
to a chemist to analyze the brick
and make sure that it is O. K.
The brick is switched before leaving, during the ride, or after they
get to the chemist. The last-named
is a confederate, and he makes a
fake test of the brass brick which
confirms the tests made by the
dupe, so the sucker trots off with
his brass brick.

Double-Crossing the Bunco Men

Another favorite method is for
the bunco men to get their victim
to a hotel where he is stopping. He
is due to leave town shortly and
some pretext is made to get him
from his room long enough for the
man with the phoney brick to enter
and exchange satchels.

A story has been told of some
gold brick swindlers who met with
more than they expected. The victim knew their game and took the

gold brick to his hotel. He went in his room, locked the door, and tried the door of the room adjoining, while his friend the swindler, was downstairs. The door was open, and the supposed sucker found the duplicate satchel with the brass brick. So he switched the satchels for himself, putting the real gold brick in the other room.

When the swindler returned, the supposed dupe left the room for a few moments. This gave the swindler his chance to exchange the satchels. Results: the victim walked away with the gold brick, and the swindler took the brass one back to his gang.

Exit the Gold Brick

The halcyon days of the gold brick game are past. This swindle was worked time and again by experts who laid their plans carefully beforehand and were so clever in their methods that they put it across. Gold bricks became so notorious that the mere mention of one makes a man hold his pocketbook and watch his bank account. Hence the old game is seldom, if ever, worked today. But there are other frauds and swindles which are just as effective.

The Violin Fraud

The Story of a Stradivarius Swindle

UNSUSPECTING storekeepers often become the victims of bunco men who plan their schemes well beforehand. The violin fraud illustrates this in detail.

Among the patrons of a small store is a poor musician who comes in frequently and makes the acquaintance of the man behind the counter. This is generally a small but prosperous store, which handles musical instruments as well as other merchandise.

The musician runs up a small bill at the store and one day he walks in carefully carrying a violin in its case. He draws the store-

The musician leaves his cherished violin with the storekeeper.

keeper aside, tells him that he wants to make a small purchase, but he has no money, although he will have in a few days. He asks if he can leave his cherished violin as security. As the bill only amounts to a few dollars the storekeeper is willing. The musician tells him to take good care of the violin as it is quite valuable, although he has no idea of its exact worth.

The violin is placed behind the counter or in a showcase. The musician takes care that it is put in a place where it can be seen but will not be handled.

A few hours later a prosperous gentleman strolls into the store. He has been there a few times before and he nods to the storekeeper. Suddenly his eye catches the violin left by the musician. He asks to see the instrument and he goes into ecstasies.

"A wonderful violin!" he exclaims. "A genuine Old Master! Where did you get it? How much will you sell it for?"

The storekeeper explains that the violin is not for sale; that it does not belong to him, but that he will find out about selling it from the musician.

The gentleman is disappointed. He is leaving town for a few days and wants the violin; in fact, he will pay up to five hundred dollars for it. But, of course, he appreciates that the storekeeper must not sell the violin without permission.

The man behind the counter states that he will tell the musician and have him wait to see the prospective buyer. The man agrees to this, but he adds that he does not want to run any risk of losing the treasure. He says that if the storekeeper can possibly keep the violin there to do so; that he will be willing to pay well for it, and that if the storekeeper, who knows the musician, can buy the violin for a reasonable sum, he will be only too glad to give the storekeeper a tidy profit on the deal.

He concludes by saying that mu-

sicians are peculiar people and rarely part with cherished instruments to strangers; that he has missed several chances to pick up good instruments because of this, and that if the storekeeper can co-operate in any way, he will make it worth his while.

Two days later the musician comes in, gloomy and morose. Before the mild-mannered storekeeper has a chance to tell him about the man who wants the violin the musician begins a tale of woe: the money he has expected has not come in, he owes rent and is generally out of luck. Nothing for him to do but sell the old violin.

The sympathetic storekeeper tells him about the man who saw the violin and who is coming back for it. But the musician can't wait. He is sure he can sell the violin for seventy-five dollars and he must have the money today. He is willing to make the sacrifice and he will take his fiddle and peddle it on the street if necessary. He

will thank the man who buys it as a friend and benefactor.

The storekeeper has an eye to business and profit. He forgets his conservatism and offers to help the musician. He brings out seventy-five dollars and buys the violin. The musician overwhelms him with thanks and goes on his way rejoicing.

The storekeeper thinks he is sitting pretty. He holds the valuable violin and waits for the customer to return. But he never does. When the storekeeper finally tries to dispose of the instrument he finds that he has been stung. It is worth just about ten dollars.

The gentleman and the musician are bunco men who work together. They pull the same flim-flam on different storekeepers in different localities, and make sixty-five dollars or more on every deal. Imitations of old violins are cheap and the average person cannot tell them from the originals.

Selling a Business

How a Pretended Grocer Sought and Found an Easy Mark

EVERY year thousands of businesses change hands. Whenever a small transaction is made the buyer takes a chance and sometimes he makes out well. But other times he may be the victim of a well-planned frame-up—an out-and-out swindle that is devised for his special benefit.

Here is a true story of a grocery business that was sold under false pretenses. It represents but one of the many schemes whereby the bunco men pick up easy money.

A man advertised that he had a grocery business for sale; he had to leave the city to go into another enterprise and would sell the business cheap.

A prospective customer became interested. The grocery man did all his work from a wagon, using a small and inexpensive stockroom. He showed his victim how the business was supposed to stand and explained that it brought regular and constant profits. The business could be bought for the cost of stock, the horse and wagon, and one thousand dollars in cash for "good will," which included a route on which the grocery man was known.

The customer was all ready to buy, and to clinch the deal the grocery man told him that he would take him over the route. If he was then satisfied, the business

The driver sold a wagon load of groceries in one trip.

would be his. If not, the deal was off.

All details of the transaction were arranged in full. The wagon was loaded with groceries, all arranged in baskets from an order sheet. Both men got in the wagon and away they started.

The driver followed a well-chosen route, passing certain houses and stopping at others. Wherever he stopped he took out the proper basket, left the wagon and went in the house. Then he reappeared with the empty basket. Sometimes he remained longer than others, taking new orders. At the end of the ride nearly all of his groceries had been delivered and he had long lists of orders to be delivered the next day. He had stopped at houses where he left no baskets, and from nearly every one he brought a good list of orders.

The customer was satisfied. The business was bought for cash and the next day the new man set out to deliver his orders. But everywhere he went he found that he was unknown. His orders were not claimed. He met with arguments and queries, and when he finished his tumultuous day he realized that all he had was the horse, wagon and stock, with no route and no territory. He had paid a thousand dollars for nothing!

The method of this swindle was absurdly simple. That was why it was so effective. All the seller had was the horse, wagon and supply of groceries, which he had picked up and kept ready for the prospective customer. The trip over the route was reserved for the first man who showed the cash.

At every house where he stopped the supposed grocery man picked out a basket and went in the back door. If the door was open, he quickly dumped the groceries and left. If a maid was there, he announced that he had the groceries that were ordered and left them before she could object.

Whenever he encountered an intelligent maid or the mistress of the house he stated that he was over-stocked on groceries, was going out of business and was offering bargain prices. He made his charge so ridiculously low that the goods were invariably purchased. Of course, he made out order lists that were phoney and the upshot of the whole trip was that he disposed of one hundred dollars' worth of groceries with virtually no return. But it paved the way to a thousand dollars of easy money from the victim.

The bunco man offers gold watches at three dollars apiece.

Sales Swindle

ONE of the slickest selling games practiced today is a watch-selling swindle that is practiced in cities as well as at county fairs. It is a game that works because the bunco man knows it and his victim does not—so the gyp artist is always a jump ahead of the sucker. Watch out for this one!

The bunco man may be located anywhere—on a sidewalk, in a small store or near the midway of a county fair. His supposed mis-

sion is to inspire confidence. He is making no surprising promises—he is merely selling "good" gold-filled watches at the special price of three dollars as a means of advertising or disposing of excess stock. The watches are worth ten dollars each, according to the salesman, who exhibits one of the time-pieces and explains its merits.

In a few minutes he has a customer. A man hands him three dollars as payment for the watch. The bunco man places the three

dollars on the table beside him and lays the watch upon it, reserving that watch for the purchaser.

Three or four other customers appear and soon there is a row of watches, each covering three dollars in cash.

The beneficent salesman is about to deliver the watches when he suddenly stops and counts the number in the row. Then he spreads his arms in a big-hearted manner and says:

"Gentlemen! Here are five of you who have confidence in me and who know a real bargain when you see it. To show you that I appreciate this I am going to give you each a ten-dollar watch for two dollars instead of three! We want these watches to go to reliable men who will appreciate them and help us to advertize them."

He picks up a watch and the three dollars beneath it. He holds them toward the first purchaser and says: "Have you five dollars? Let me see it!"

The victim brings out a five-dollar bill and the bunco man takes it in his left hand, holding the watch and three dollars in his right.

"There!" says the gyp. "Five dollars takes the watch and the three one-dollar bills. Three dollars in cash and the watch for a five spot. Three from five is two—and you get the watch for two dollars!"

He lays the five-dollar bill on the table and puts the watch and the three dollars on it. Then he turns to the next man and makes him the same offer with a chance to save a dollar.

In this way he forms the row of watches again, with each watch covering eight dollars. If any customer does not have five dollars, the bunco man shakes his head sadly and says: "You don't want the three dollars? All right, then you just get the watch."

Now he looks at his customers and points to the watches.

"Gentlemen," he says, "I just made this offer to you to find out which of you would be good, reliable men—the kind of men we want to help us in our big campaign.''

He picks up a watch and the eight dollars with it.

''Here,'' he says, ''is a ten-dollar watch and eight dollars. I will give you this watch for one dollar! Give me nine dollars and take the watch and the money. Think of it! A ten-dollar watch for one dollar. This is your big chance!''

The first purchaser immediately puts up nine dollars. He gets the watch and the eight dollars, which are promptly handed to him. The others do the same and the bunco man distributes watch chains to the ''lucky'' persons as souvenirs of the occasion.

Many intelligent people have fallen for this game without ever realizing the swindle. The artful bunco man leads them to believe that they are getting something for almost nothing—in reality they are *buying back their own money!*

The three dollars that he offers for five—with the watch—is the three dollars the customer put up; the eight dollars that he gives for nine also belongs to the victim. The result is that the sucker hands out nine dollars for the watch, which is not worth more than two with the chain included.

The bunco man makes a fair profit on the men who pay three dollars for the watch and then quit. Sometimes a victim cannot put up more than the five called for on the second offer. In that case he gets the watch and his own three dollars for the five, so the gyp makes five dollars on the sale.

When this game is worked with watches the first customer is usually a confederate or ''shill,'' who falls for the game without hesitation. This leads on the suckers.

In actual practice a glib talker puts this swindle across every time he tries it. It is just deceptive **enough to fool the customers.**

Panhandling De Luxe

The Silver Tongued Swindler Who Runs No Risk

EVERYONE has probably been subjected to pan-handlers—those ill-clad waifs of fortune who shamble along the streets at night and try to touch kindhearted people.

''Say, Mister, will you give me the price of a meal? I ain't had nuthin' to eat for two days.''

That is a familiar plea often heard. Perhaps the man needs a meal—maybe he is just thirsty and wants a drink; but at any event, he is probably hard up or out of luck or he would not stoop to such a petty request. These fellows are running the risk of arrest for vagrancy and they get more cold looks than cold cash.

But watch out for the pan-handler de luxe—the aristocrat of the bums. There are plenty of them and they make an easy living by preying upon credulous victims.

A young business man is walking home along a well-lighted street. He encounters a middle-aged man of gentlemanly appearance who stops him, as though to ask the way to some destination.

''Pardon me,'' says the stranger, ''but I have an unusual request to make of you. Are you a good judge of human nature?''

The young man looks puzzled.

''Why, yes,'' he replies, ''I suppose I am.''

''Well, how would you judge me?'' continues the stranger. ''Do I look honest and reliable?''

''Why, yes,'' replies the young man.

''I thought you would say that,'' replies the stranger. ''I am something of a judge of human nature, too, and I could tell by your looks that you are a reliable and trustworthy young man. Otherwise I would have hesitated to speak to you.''

The young man has sized the stranger up by this time. He takes him for a professor or a Sunday-school superintendent. The stranger is well dressed, but quiet in appearance with a fatherly look that breathes confidence.

''I find it very difficult to speak further,'' says the stranger, ''but I know that I would feel no offence if someone would come to me with the request I have to make; and so I am taking the same liberty with you.

''I have been here in town for several days. I found it necessary to stay longer than I expected and, much to my chagrin, I have discovered that I am temporarily out of funds.

''My relatives are in Washington and I have tried to communicate with them, but they are out of town and will not be back until Monday. It is now Saturday night and here I am without money. I make it a point never to carry valuables, and so I have no means of obtaining meals or lodging for tonight and tomorrow.''

The young man's sympathies are aroused.

''I'd like to help you out,'' he says slowly.

''If you can,'' replies the stranger, ''you will obtain my sincere gratitude. Being a stranger here I do not know where to go or how economically I can live for two days. Perhaps you—''

The young man is figuring.

''I can let you have ten dollars,'' he begins, then he looks at the well-dressed stranger and feels cheap because he has made so small an offer. ''Or perhaps fifteen. That will enable you to live here until you hear from your relations.''

''I would like to get back to Washington,'' replies the stranger.

"Here's twenty dollars—will that be enough?"

young man with a smile. "I know how I'd feel in the same fix. Good-night and good luck. I know I'll hear from you."

He goes on his way cheerfully. He recalls that he does not know the stranger's name—but what does that matter? He will hear from him in a few days and there is a real satisfaction in helping the other fellow.

But the stranger thinks otherwise. Out of sight around the corner he chuckles to himself and laughs when he realizes how easy the old game is after all.

This story may sound exaggerated, but it is not. As a bunco game it is psychologically a success. It scores a bull's-eye nearly every time and it is a game that few people suspect.

It is worked with variations in many cities. Watch out for it. If a man approaches you with his tale of woe and says, "I come from Washington and—" take no pity upon his gray hairs and the sublimity of his countenance. Just reply,

"I'm from Omaha. Let's team together and say we're from Honolulu. Maybe we can pick up some real money."

Try it and see if the stranger waits to say good-bye.

This little story shows that the ways and means of the bunco men are many. The real experts stick to one game and play it to perfection. Appearances are deceitful—when the bunco man is around. The only way to detect the smooth bunco artist is to listen closely to his story and lead him on. The better his tale sounds the flimsier is it likely to be. The man who always has a good reason and a quick reply bears watching. These fellows think it all out beforehand and they are always one step ahead of their questioners.

The experts who make an easy living by this sort of flim-flam employ different stories to suit the time, place and occasion. They get plenty of suckers. Don't be one!

"Once I am there I can assure you that you will receive the money by the first mail."

"Oh, I don't doubt that," responds the young man quickly, hoping not to injure the stranger's feelings. "Suppose I give you twenty—then you can go to a fairly good hotel and leave for home when you are ready."

"I would appreciate it," replies the stranger hesitatingly. "At the same time I feel that to impose upon you—of course you understand how I feel about this—"

The young man produces two ten-dollar bills and hands them to him.

"I certainly thank you," says the stranger. "Have you a card? I must have your name and address."

He receives the card, reads it carefully so as not to forget it and places it carefully in his pocket.

"This does indeed give me confidence in human nature," he says in tones of gratitude. "I had not intended to keep you so long. Thank you again."

"That's all right," says the

Methods of "Short Changers" Exposed

SHORT-CHANGE men are the parasites of every outdoor amusement. Gamesters and gamblers spend their time and money creating devices to separate the "sucker" from his cash, but the short-change man, relying only on his nerve and quick thinking, reaps his harvest of nickels, dimes and dollars unknown to his victims.

You will see the short-change man at the ticket booth on a carnival lot; sometimes he is found in the amusement parks, and occasionally he will appear behind the counter of a store. His job is to serve the public and he makes the public serve him.

The easiest method employed by the short-changer is simply to deliver change for $1 to everyone who gives him a bill for a higher denomination. In a rush past a ticket booth such a plan will often succeed. If it is noticed and protested, the short-changer apologizes and gives the customer the additional change.

But short-changers do not like to hear "squawks" from their victims, so they generally employ methods that pass unnoticed.

When a large bill is given to an expert short-changer he may employ the folded-bill trick. Suppose he receives $10. He picks up a stack of one-dollar bills and counts off nine by lifting the ends one at a time. He hands the bills to the customer and with it change in coin. Nothing could be fairer.

But the customer receives seven dollar bills instead of nine. Two of the bills are folded across the center, so when the short-changer counts nine he counts two of the bills twice.

In handing the pile of bills to the customer he cleverly straightens the folded bills and all trace of the swindle is gone.

The most popular form of short-changing is called "take it or leave it." The procedure is as follows: The ticket man counts out a pile of change, making sure that the customer sees the amount is correct. He performs this operation near a large pile of change which is scattered on the counter.

He sets his hand on the money he has counted and pushes it to the customer. Under cover of his hand he separates the money into two groups so that when he raises his hand several coins are left a little distance behind the others.

The customer takes the pile nearest to him and, thinking that the rest is not his, walks away. If he happens to count his money and finds it short he returns, and when he starts to raise a protest the short-changer looks at the counter, points to the few coins lying there, and says: "There is the rest of

Every night the short change artist takes his share of illegitimate gain.

your change. I gave it to you— why didn't you take it?"

A similar method is sometimes employed by operators of shooting galleries and game counters. They

"Take it or leave it." While the fingers push some of the coins forward, the thumb retains others.

lay down the player's change while he is occupied with the game and say nothing more. If the customer picks it up, all right. If he doesn't, it remains there, and the operator picks it up later on. Sometimes the counters are dark and the money cannot be seen. At the end of the evening the operator will brush his hand along the counter and pick up plenty of dimes and nickels.

A ticket seller stationed in a booth with a regular ticket window can work the "take it or leave it" system with ease. He pushes the change forward with one hand, but lets the odd coins remain behind the post beside the ticket window where they are out of sight of the customer. In case the man counts his money and comes back he will see the coins that belong to him and the ticket seller often pushes them farther into view. Then the customer will not suspect the ticket seller. But he seldom comes back.

Booths of this sort are usually seen at amusement parks and the ticket seller who operates the short-change game takes good account of the angles of vision, pushing the coins behind the post on the most convenient side.

Short-changers have a way of

making remarks that hurry customers along and cause them to neglect to count their change. They rely upon various schemes at which they are extremely clever.

A man selling tickets works this gag: He has a bag of dimes and he is selling ten-cent tickets. Along comes a customer who puts down a dollar and asks for one ticket.

The short-changer lays a ticket on the counter and says: "Ten." Then counting dimes he continues, "Twenty, thirty, forty, fifty, sixty, seventy, eighty, ninety—and the ticket is one dollar."

His game is counting the ticket twice—as the first ten cents and the last dime. Many short-changers have used this swindle regularly.

How a folded bill is counted twice.

It brings small return, but on a big night, when lots of dollar bills are in sight, the swindler will take in a lot of extra change.

When he sees a chance to take in more the short-changer does not neglect it. One of the swiftest swindles is that of changing a five-dollar bill into quarters. The bunco man makes one dollar on every transaction.

Where the Swindle Comes In

Here is the method: He puts the five-dollar bill into a cash drawer and, picking up a handful of quarter dollars, counts them out, saying: "One, two, three, four—one dollar"; then, counting four more,

"twenty-five, fifty, seventy-five, two dollars"; then, counting four more, "one, two, three, *four*"— with an accent on the last word. Then he picks up more quarters and continues where he left off: "Four twenty-five, fifty, seventy-five, five dollars!"

Read this lingo over rapidly and you will see how he omitted the count of three dollars entirely. The ruse is seldom noticed. If the customer decides to count his change, the sharper is ready for him. He picks up a dollar bill from the back of the counter as soon as he sees the victim looking at the quarters. When the man raises his head to protest the short-changer smiles sweetly and says:

"You have four dollars in quarters—and one dollar more makes five!"

The boldest short-changers "hold out" money when they make change. One of these swindlers counts change into his left hand; then he slides the change into his right and gives it to the customer. In letting the money slip into his right hand he retains two or three coins in the left so that the victim gets less than he is entitled to. If the customer raises a kick, the short-changer says: "Let's see what I gave you."

He takes the change in his right hand, and in transferring it to the

How the short change artist holds out coins.

left naturally adds it to the coins he has kept hidden in the left hand. Then he patiently counts the coins again and shows the victim that the change was correct.

After that he gives the change back to the victim and in so doing "holds out" some of the coins again. The customer will never count the money a second time as he feels cheap because he thinks he has made a mistake.

Short-changing is one of the biggest swindles in America today. It is a petty graft, as far as the individual is concerned, but there are so many working it that collectively it assumes gigantic proportions. It is sometimes difficult to detect the short-changers at work, but the man who is fore-warned against them can always count his change and stick right there until he gets the correct amount. A few thousand vigilant customers can crimp the swindler's game.

Watch out for short-changers and save your money!

Inside Information on Jam Auctions

All About the Celebrated Pitch Game—
Its History and Its Development

YEARS ago when bunco men needed money they had a little game which never failed to work. By way of introduction we will set the scene back near the end of the nineteenth century in the main street of the little town of Blanksville.

A flashy buckboard drives into town. One man is in front, another in back. The carriage comes to a stop near the principal corner —no traffic cops in those days, so it stays there. The man in back stands up, opens a satchel and begins to talk to the crowd that quickly assembles.

"Gentlemen," he says, "here are some nice souvenir purses. I am giving these out to lucky customers. All I ask is a dime from each of you. Every man who gives me a dime gets a purse and I guarantee he will be satisfied."

Up come the dimes and two dozen hands each receive a purse.

"Worth a dime, isn't it?" says the bunco man. "Everyone that is satisfied hold up his hand!"

Up go two dozen hands. The bunco man smiles. In each hand he places a dime, returning the money to the satisfied customers.

"How's that?" he asks. "Everybody has his dime and a pocketbook too. I want you all to be satisfied!"

From his bag he takes some leather wallets.

"A dollar for each of these wallets," he says. "Just ten of them here. Who's first? Remember, I guarantee satisfaction!"

Ten persons hand in a dollar each.

"Satisfied?" asks the bunco man.

Up go the ten hands and each one gets a dollar back. A murmur of surprise goes through the crowd. The lucky persons are congratulated.

"Here is another!" announces the bunco man. "A fine gold watch and chain! Look it over. I have some of these here. Who'll give me ten dollars for a watch? Remember, I guarantee satisfaction!"

The glittering gold watch looks like a fine gift. The crowd surges around the rear of the buckboard, everyone anxious to get his watch before the supply gives out. Twenty watches are distributed in this manner. The bunco man holds the money, and the eager recipients hold the watches.

The bunco man looks upon the crowd with a philanthropic smile. He spreads the ten-dollar bills and holds them in his outstretched hand.

"Everybody that is satisfied hold up a hand!" he says.

A score of hands are raised expectantly.

"All satisfied?" asks the bunco man. "That's good. Remember, I always guarantee satisfaction!"

The man in front snaps the whip, the bunco man drops to his seat and pockets the ten-dollar bills while the buckboard whirls away. The victims look at one another in astonishment. They have paid ten dollars apiece for their watches —flashy, gaudy, but worthless timepieces that cost the bunco man ten dollars a dozen!

With the coming of the automobile this old bunco game dwindled away. Sleepy towns became enlivened cities and pursuit of the bunco men was made possible. So the scene shifted to the city and there it may be seen today, flourishing as long as the police will permit it, but in a new and alluring guise. The inhabitants of the metropolis fall for the old swindle as easily as the natives of the hamlet, although many of the victims of the new style game are rural folk who are visiting the city.

A small store is opened on a busy street. A man stands outside amusing the crowd with tricks. Soon a respectable gathering is on hand.

The man in front of the store wraps up a dozen dollar bills and puts them in a box. Then he picks up some small envelopes and addresses the crowd.

"Before I make the dollar bills disappear from the envelope I will give out souvenirs. Each of these envelopes contains an article of merchandise. Who will buy an envelope for a cent?"

A dozen persons risk a cent apiece. The man lays the envelopes and the pennies on his little table and continues.

"Before I give out these envelopes I will ask you all to step inside. I can't crowd up the street. Walk right in, please."

He carries his table back into the store and the curious crowd follows. He takes his position behind a counter and points to an array of plated silver sugar bowls, military brushes, cigarette cases and other articles.

"All these articles," he announces, "will be given away for five cents each! This is our advertising plan. We do not advertise in street cars or in newspapers. We give away merchandise. In order to do this we must run an auction and have bids on the articles. But all you pay for any article is five cents!"

He points to a man and says: "You say one."

The person replies, "One."

Another man is told to say "two," another "three," another "four" and another "five."

"Sold," says the self-styled auctioneer. "Show me five!"

The man who said "five," produces a five-dollar bill.

"Keep your money," says the auctioneer. "Give me a nickel."

He lays the nickel in the sugar bowl and points to the different articles.

"Who will say five on these?" he asks.

Several persons immediately say "five." The auctioneer asks to see the fives. Some of them exhibit five-dollar bills, but in every case the auctioneer simply takes a nic-

kel. He puts a coin on each article. Then he hands the sugar bowl, the brushes and all other articles to the persons who spoke up and returns each one his nickel.

He then centers his attention upon the persons who were quickest to respond—the ones who showed him the five-dollar bills. He draws them to the back of the shop to see some more articles, and another auctioneer tells the rest of the crowd to move along—that a special sale is about to be conducted. In this way the crowd dwindles. The penny souvenirs are distributed, each one being a small, cheap pin.

The chief auctioneer shows a large closed box and asks for bids on it. Again people say "one," "two," "three," "four" and "five."

This time he says, "Show me the five dollars." The man who said "five" obliges, and the five dollars is placed under the box.

"You say five?" says the auctioneer, pointing to another man. The victim responds and his five dollars is taken by the auctioneer and placed beneath a box. In this way the three or four customers who remain each have five dollars on the table under a box.

"Here," says the auctioneer, "is a genuine diamond ring priced at seventy dollars. Who will say five?"

One man says "five." Another is told to say "ten," a third "fifteen" and a fourth "twenty." The lucky man who said "twenty" is told to show twenty dollars, which he does, and it is placed beneath the diamond ring.

The other persons are each asked to say "twenty." They do so and each one shows twenty dollars, which is placed with a diamond ring just like the first.

The auctioneer repeats this with a gold watch and with a diamond stick-pin. So one man has sixty-five dollars on the counter covered by different articles. The second man is similarly situated, and if the others have sixty-five dollars

with them, they are in the same boat. If their limit is five, twenty-five or forty-five, the auctioneer leaves them out after they have put up all their money on various articles and are waiting to receive the merchandise with the money back.

But now a strange thing happens.

"This," says the auctioneer, "concludes the sale."

He hands the first man the closed box which is opened to show a smoking set or a manicure set. He gives him the ring, the watch and the stick-pin. A chain is given with the watch, a pie-knife with the ring, and silver spoons with the stick-pin.

Each of the other persons is treated likewise—in accordance with the amount of money they have put up. Then the auctioneer gathers up all the money, sweeps it into a cash box behind the counter and walks to the front of the store, followed by the puzzled victims. There he gives each one another article of merchandise as a special souvenir and he walks out front to raise another crowd.

Then it dawns upon the victims that they have been "sold." They try to question the auctioneer, but he is busy with the next sale. They walk back into the store and talk to another man who points out the merits of the merchandise and writes out so-called guarantees for the watch and the ring. If they still have doubts, they are taken to an appraiser who lauds the value of the jewelry. The first man who put up sixty-five dollars expresses his satisfaction and congratulates himself on the bargains he has made. This leads the others to do likewise and they leave the store with their doubts soothed.

The total wholesale value of sixty-five dollars' worth of merchandise that is foisted upon an unsuspecting customer in one of these jam auctions is probably less than ten dollars. The whole affair is not an auction at all—it is a smooth-working bunco game.

"You say twenty? All right, show me twenty dollars, and put it here with the watch."

The man who is so quick to show his money is a confederate, known technically as a "capper," and in slang as a "shill." He is hired by the house and he is provided with plenty of money before the sale begins. The suckers follow him like a row of ducks when the gander marches to a pond.

When the victims start to squawk for their money the shill stays with them and wants to know if he has received value. Every argument satisfies him and that influences the suckers.

If a man puts up a fight for his money, the manager comes out and threatens to have him arrested for bidding at a legitimate auction and then refusing to pay for what he has bought. If this doesn't scare him away, the manager takes the

sucker in a back room and makes an adjustment, giving him back ten or fifteen dollars, or taking back part of the merchandise.

The whole game is a flim-flam from beginning to end. The merchandise that is given away does not cost more than five or six dollars, although it is flashy. The watches are worth less than two dollars each, and the rings less than five.

The auctioneer can give out ten free souvenirs, a smoking set, a ring, a watch and a stick-pin and make about fifty dollars clear profit on the sixty-five he takes from a sucker.

On a good day these stores can run more than a dozen sales. Sometimes they draw blanks, but if they get a half a dozen suckers during

the course of a day they will clear from $200 to $600, and on some days the returns will be greater. If one sucker falls for the game and flashes a big bankroll, the auctioneers will get him in the back of the store and sell him a diamond which they value at $500 for a price like $175 and he will leave the place happy, carrying a ring that is worth between $20 and $50.

A game like this is not a legitimate auction at all, and many cities have ordinances barring such swindles. In other towns they are allowed to continue unmolested and the auctioneers often threaten a protesting victim with arrest.

In New York, the greatest city of them all, where people are wise enough to know better, the jam auctions have done a big business. They are barred from that city, but occasionally a pitch game breaks loose, and when it does the swindlers have more nerve than anywhere else.

Here is the story of a pitch game in New York, which was run without any pretense of an auction.

A crowd was drawn into a store after watching a midget cutting silly capers on the sidewalk. The proprietor brought out a lot of thimbles and said, "Who's sport enough to put up a dime?"

He took in a couple of dollars in dimes, handed out the thimbles and gave the money back. He repeated this with other small articles, getting varying amounts and always returning the money. When he had boosted the game to a dollar he ran out of souvenirs so he said:

"Let's all be sports and put up five dollars apiece. No souvenirs left, so I'll give each man a match to show that he has put up five bucks. No—a match is worth something, so I'll give each man the broken half of a match."

The crowd by this time expected anything—except what they were going to get. About twenty men put up five dollars apiece, and each received a broken match in return. Then they waited to get their money back, with some sort of a present besides.

The bunco man walked to the back of the store and said:

"Each gentleman has received something for his five dollars, and as we have no more souvenirs the distribution is ended." Then he walked out the back way, leaving the crowd in an empty store with nothing to take away with them.

What did they do? Nothing! They looked at each other sheepishly and left the store. No man likes to admit that he is a sucker, and their pride was worth more to them than five dollars.

In this instance everyone knew that he had been swindled, but in the regulation jam auction the men in the store are open for business all the time and they generally fool their victims into believing that they have received wonderful value for their money. Many a small-town sheik has gone to a big city and has carted away a suitcase full of worthless junk which he has brought home and proudly exhibited as proof of his ability as a bargain finder. If someone told

him that his $50 watch and $100 diamond ring were worth a few dollars at wholesale, he wouldn't believe it. When a man dwells in blissful ignorance he seldom has sense enough to become wise.

Many jam auctions are licensed as auction houses. In some cases they make use of the names of defunct concerns and thus are enabled to appear as recognized organizations.

They do not always swindle people in the bold manner explained before. There are certain localities where people with money are plentiful and the bunco men find that they can make prfit by running what appears to be a bona fide sale —to the uninitiated.

For example: the auctioneer gathers a crowd into his shop and brings out five or six of the cheap gold watches that look so good. He explains that these were purchased from a pawnshop in Chicago and that they are fine, valuable watches that will be sacrificed. He asks for bids and the cappers run the price

up to nine or ten dollars. Then one of the suckers makes a bid and gets a watch. Every time the auctioneer makes a profit of from six to eight dollars; then he offers other articles on the same basis. The customers think they are getting bargains; but if none of them bids high enough to suit the auctioneer, his capper steps in and makes the highest bid.

A legitimate auction house would never attempt anything of this sort. A reliable firm disposes of goods which must be sold and collects a commission for the service. Cappers are illegal in many places, and any store employing them is liable to lose its license.

But the bunco men, in their quest for inflated profits, will resort to any illegal methods—if they can get away with them. They pull the same old story every time the crowd changes. They are parasites who interfere with legitimate firms, and they spring up time and again, despite all efforts to suppress them.

Endless Chains

ONE of the commonest methods of undesirable merchandising is known as the "endless chain." In its simplest form it is merely faulty and illogical; when worked to its fullest extent it becomes an absolute flim-flam.

Here is a typical example used some years ago:

Booklets were sold at a dollar apiece. Each booklet contained three coupons, which the purchaser sold to his friends at twenty-five cents apiece. Each coupon counted as a twenty-five-cent payment on a dollar booklet.

As soon as the purchasers of the coupons had bought booklets the man who took the original booklet was given a premium that was actually worth one dollar and twenty-five cents. In brief, his final expenditure was only twenty-five cents, and he received a dollar more than that in value! His friends who purchased coupons and booklets could do the same.

This looked good. A dollar for nothing!

The men who operated the endless chain were always ahead of the game. They received a dollar from the original purchaser and seventy-five cents from each of his three friends, a total of three dollars and a quarter before they paid out a dollar and a quarter. They were two dollars ahead on every deal!

Money can't be made from nothing. Someone had to get stung. When a scheme like this has swept through a community it dies out, leaving thousands of unredeemed coupons. The promoters and the early purchasers make money—the others hold the bag.

The Jewelry Swindle

Where the Bunco Man Invokes Legal Aid

THERE are certain swindles which are unusually dangerous, inasmuch as the bunco men arrange matters so that they are able to bring action against other people. They play with fire when they attempt such games, for if they are detected it will go hard with them. For this reason they carefully arrange their plans beforehand.

These are not general swindles, but are usually specific instances, where the crook builds up an alibi for himself, and leaves no detail uncared for. Here is a typical story that illustrates the methods of the arch-swindler.

A well-dressed man entered a jewelry store in a certain city. He asked to see some watches, and he became interested in a handsome timepiece that was priced at $50. He explained to the jeweler that he had only a few dollars with him and that, as it was just past noon on Saturday, it was too late for him to go to the bank. So he offered to buy the watch if the jeweler would accept his check in payment.

The jeweler looked the man over; decided that he was O. K., and took the check. The patron departed with the watch and strolled nonchalantly into a barber shop next door. That marked the end of Scene I.

The barber's story aroused the jeweler's suspicions. He demanded an explanation from the man who bought the watch.

The second stanza took place in the barber shop. During the course of a haircut the man who had bought the watch started a conversation with the barber. He asked him if he would like to buy a good watch at a bargain—a $50 watch for $30. Whether or not the barber was greatly interested, the man grew insistent. He showed the watch to the barber and knocked the price down to $25. Then he told the barber to take the watch in to the jeweler and find out its actual value. While the man was putting on his coat and adjusting his necktie the barber, now an interested and prospective customer —and also curious—left the shop in charge of an assistant and went into the jewelry store.

There he showed the watch to the proprietor. This scene was short but active. The jeweler thought of his check; he saw the man's game in a jiffy. Buy a watch for $50, using a phoney check. Sell the watch for $25 and make $25. Learning that the man was still in the barber shop, the jeweler decided to act promptly and crimp his little game.

The picture illustrates Scene IV. A stormy argument outside of the jewelry store. The man who bought the watch is at the left, the jeweler in the center and the barber on the right. The jeweler is getting the barber's testimony. Here is what transpired.

The jeweler demanded to know why the man tried to sell the watch for half price just after he had bought it. The purchaser declared that he needed $25 very badly, as he was leaving town in a few hours, and he showed a railroad ticket and Pullman reservation to prove it. His ticket, he said, had cost him more than he expected. Sitting in the barber chair, he had decided that ready cash was worth more to him than the watch.

The jeweler wanted to know why he didn't bring the watch back;

Souvenir Schemes

VARIOUS cities have become the centers of operation for souvenir schemes that are largely a form of misrepresentation.

A person receives an attractive circular advertising a set of toilet preparations, with an itemized list of the retail value of each article. The total value is given as from $10 to $15.

The circular states that these sets will be given away, the only charge being made to cover expenses of shipping, distribution and bringing the plan to the attention of the public. The person who takes advantage of the offer pays a price ranging from $1.75 to $2.25 for the complete set valued at nearly $15.

This is far less than half of the wholesale price and many people send in their orders. The sets are sometimes displayed in a local store with the retail price attached.

These souvenir schemes are made possible by value inflation. Investigations have proved that the toilet preparations are cheap and misrepresented, and that their retail value is approximately $1.00. The promoters realize a tidy profit and the victims, instead of receiving a bargain, pay double for the merchandise.

Better Business Bureaus in various cities have worked actively against these souvenir schemes, which are real swindles because of their misrepresentation.

When a recognized product is offered at a special price, through an advertising campaign, it is worth buying. But beware of the "fly-by-nights" that you never heard of before and never will hear of again.

the man said that he couldn't explain why, but after all, he thought he would prefer to take the watch. So he quickly snatched the watch from the barber, said that he had to leave for his train, and started down the street.

That meant quick action on the part of the jeweler and his friend, the barber. They followed the man excitedly, demanding the watch. The man said that it was his own property and that he would keep it. The altercation brought a policeman on the scene, and the man was arrested, accused by the jeweler of passing a bad check.

The presence of the policeman subdued the man who bought the watch. He argued for a few minutes, but his manner convinced all present that he was guilty, and he was taken to the station house. There he was held in custody. It was some hours before he could communicate with friends and arrange his release through a lawyer.

On Monday morning, when the bank opened, the check was cashed. The man proved to be a regular depositor who always maintained a sizable account. The jeweler received his money and the man had the watch.

Then came the epilogue. The man brought suit against the jeweler for false arrest. He proved that he had missed an important engagement through his detention. Everything was in his favor. The jeweler had accepted the check without question, and having sold the watch had no right to interfere with the subsequent actions of the purchaser. It was a swindle; but the planning and execution put the jeweler in a fix and made the man who bought the watch the injured party.

Many flim-flams of this sort are put over by clever bunco men who build up a case against an honest and well-meaning merchant and then invoke the aid of a shrewd lawyer.

The Chinese merchant carried the lamp up the walk.

Swindling Storekeepers

A Confidence Game Used On Unsuspecting Merchants

MERCHANTS and store-keepers are frequently swindled by bunco artists who work up elaborate schemes with which to dupe their victims. Here is the story of a game that has been used more than once, and it is told as it actually was operated in an Eastern city.

A well-dressed women called at a store owned by a Chinese merchant. The shop was stocked with many Oriental articles of high value, and the feminine customer was greatly attracted by some of the goods on display.

She began by making a few purchases; then she became interested in rugs and draperies of high value, and soon she had picked out articles that totalled well into thousands of dollars.

She explained to the proprietor that she had not intended to buy so much when she entered, that she had only a few hundred dollars with her, and that she would like to take the purchases home, so as to assure their safe delivery.

So she suggested that the proprietor himself come with her and deliver the goods, when he would be paid in full.

This sounded fine to the Chinese merchant, so the woman called her chauffeur and her expensive limousine standing outside was loaded with the valuable purchases. She sat in back surrounded by the goods, while the merchant took his seat with the chauffeur, carrying some of the merchandise.

The car drove a few miles, and drew up before the entrance to a large house in a fashionable neighborhood—the residence of the wealthy woman. The chauffeur and the Chinese alighted, and the lady passed different articles to them through the open door.

"Go ahead and ring the bell," she said to the merchant, who already had his arms full—holding a lamp and a large package. The chauffeur was also picking up bundles.

"I will bring a few of the small packages," she added, "and you can come back for more."

The happy Chinese merchant eagerly led the procession. Up the walk he went, to the marble steps, where he set down the lamp and package so that he could ring the bell. He turned to speak to the chauffeur, and his eyes opened in amazement.

Lady, chauffeur, and automobile had disappeared! Not a trace remained of them!

It was some time before the man could collect his scattered wits. Then he reported the matter to the police. It was easy to decide what had happened.

The chauffeur and the lady were accomplices—clever swindlers, who had hired an expensive car and a chauffeur's uniform. They had planned the game beforehand, and their methods had won the Chinese merchant's confidence. They had driven to a fine house by prearrangement and there they easily induced the merchant to start up the steps. Then the disguised chauffeur quickly dropped his bundles in back, leaped to the wheel and, with the motor still running, was able to speed away.

This was all done in a few seconds, and the car was out of sight before the Chinese merchant looked around.

Swindles like this are frequently carried out by clever crooks who specialized in defrauding unsuspecting merchants. They work their games in big stores and small, all according to their prearranged method of action.

Finding a Diamond

Easy Money for Everybody

LOOK out for the diamond-ring game. It has been worked time and again upon unsuspecting persons and it has many variations.

Everyone knows the thrill of finding money or valuables on the street. But did you ever experience the disappointment of having someone get there a second before you? That is the psychological factor in the diamond-ring swindle.

A man is walking down the street. He approaches a corner and suddenly he sees a glittering object. As he hastens forward to pick it up another man comes around the corner and snatches the article from under his hand.

The man who lost out is a well-dressed individual; the other is cheaply clad—a typical loafer. Nevertheless, curiosity compels the prosperous person to look at the ring which has been found.

"Tough luck, Bud," says the loafer. "This looks like a real sparkler. I hated to snatch it away from you like that."

"That's all right," says the well-dressed man. "I wonder if it is a real diamond ring?"

"Sure enough," says the loafer. "I know 'em when I see 'em. Believe me, bo, I'm goin' to cash this in for a ten-spot before somebody comes snoopin' around and lookin' for it."

"If it's a real diamond," says the gentleman, "a reward will be offered for it in excess of ten dollars. If no one claims the ring, it will be worth much more than that."

"Ten bucks is plenty for me," says the other. "I'll give it to anybody that has that much coin. I need the dough bad."

This leads the gentleman to offer ten dollars for the ring. His offer is eagerly accepted and the ring changes hands.

But perhaps the gentleman is skeptical about the matter. He is about to leave when the loafer stops him.

"Say, bud," he remarks, "maybe you're right about this here ring. It ought to be worth more than a ten-spot. But if I try to find out about it, they'll think I cribbed it somewhere. Do me a favor, will you? There's Old Jake's hock shop across the street. Take it in and ask them what it's worth."

This interests the gentleman's curiosity. He takes the ring, enters the pawn shop and asks the clerk to give him a value on the ring.

"Can't offer you nothin' on it," says the clerk, squinting at the diamond through an optical glass. "The boss is out just now and he takes care of all jewelry. I know sparklers, though, and this one looks like it was worth between three an' four hundred dollars. The old man ought to give you a couple of hundred on it."

"Thank you," says the gentleman. He leaves the shop and returns to the loafer. He tells him the good news and the finder of the ring is astounded.

"Gee, ain't that great?" he says.

As he stoops to pick up the ring, another man comes around the corner and snatches it from beneath his outstretched hand.

"Say, I'd a given it away for a ten-spot. I'm afraid to soak it, though. I might get pinched. Listen—I'll divvy with you. I need the dough. What'll you give me for the ring, an' then it's yours? Twenty-five dollars?"

This sounds soft to the enterprising gentleman. He pays twenty-five dollars for the ring and may throw in a few dollars besides. He gets the ring. The loafer gets the cash.

But when the new owner of the ring takes it to a jewelry store he finds that it is an imitation. He has been made the sucker of a bunco game.

The loafer is the swindler. He plants the ring at the corner where it will catch the eye of the victim.

Then he appears at the right instant and grabs the ring. If he can sell it for ten dollars right off, he is satisfied. If not, he induces the victim to go to the pawnshop where the clerk is in the game and gives his opinion of the matter. The loafer then divides the spoils with the clerk, who assumes no responsibility as he is not an expert on diamonds, but merely ventures his opinion when the gentleman comes in.

This is a bunco game that has been worked on many people, for it is so accidental in its setting that the average man will never suspect that he is the victim of a well-planned swindle. When you see a man find a ring in the street, let him keep it.

All About Carnival Games

"Grifters," "Gaffs," "Cappers," "Shills," "Laydowns," "Grinds," "Joints," "Flashers," "Wheels," "Bloomers," and "Red Ones"

THE carnival man has a parlance all his own. Every year the old hands at the game start on the road to invade the towns and countryside of America and make some easy money. Late spring and early summer are their happy hunting days, but the big haul comes in the early fall when the country fairs are in full bloom and the suckers throng the midway and bite like all suckers should.

Crooked carnival games have been exposed in the past, but never to any great degree. Writers who have explained the methods of the men who operate them have gone into very few details. But here the true facts are laid bare, and the reader who has lost money to these parasites will learn how he lost it and why he should leave these games alone in the future.

There is a resemblance between certain games, and as the reader looks through these games he will see how different swindles have been put to varied uses. In fact, he may find some repetition, but if he does, it will be there for the purpose of emphasis—to implant certain facts in one's mind so that they will not be forgotten.

At the same time, the reader should remember that the operators of carnival games are ingenious and that they are willing to spend money for new ideas. Even though he may learn plenty about their methods he should be careful about bucking the game—for it is hard to beat a man at his own game. The biggest suckers are those who think they know all about it. The bunco men like to see them come along.

Before reading about the games, the reader should learn something about the carnival business in general. He will be given a list of terms used by these people, so that he will know their language and will be able to understand remarks that he may chance to overhear.

Racket

The carnival business is called a "racket" by those who are in the game. They speak of the carnival "racket," and when they refer to another carnival man, they speak of him as a man who is "in the "racket."

Joint

A "joint" is a carnival game. It may be termed an "amusement device," or a game of chance or skill, by those who are talking to the public, but to those "in the racket" a carnival game is a "joint" and always will be.

Two-Way Joints

A "two-way joint" is a game that can be worked two ways—either fairly or crookedly. The man who advertises a "two-way joint" for sale is telling the prospective customer that here is a game which can be fixed against the player. Another term involves the word "strong." When a carnival man says that he has a game which can be worked "strong" he means that he has a "two-way joint."

Grifter

The "grifter" is the carnival man who operates a "two-way joint." There are plenty of these fellows loose every year. A few years ago protests were so strong against them that an association was formed to drive them out of business, and to leave no one in the field except the men who ran games that gave the player a small but appreciable chance. This plan never worked effectively. The "grifters" laid low for a time, and then blossomed out brighter than ever.

Grind-Stores

These are "joints" that operate on a small scale for nickel play, or sometimes for dimes, but always with the promise of quick turnover because of frequent and steady play. The "nickel gougers" who run such "joints" take a lot of small change from a great many people. That is where they make their profit.

Slum

This is a term used in all branches of the carnival business, and it refers to cheap articles of junk that are virtually given away as prizes. Thus a carnival operator will give every player a prize for his dime—but most of the players will receive "slum"—pins, whistles, collar buttons, etc., that are worth less than a cent apiece.

Percentage Games—Percentage Wheels

Some carnival games operate on a percentage basis. That is, a dozen players will get in the game and one is sure to win. They pay a dime apiece and the winner gets a box of candy worth thirty or forty cents, which gives the operator a big profit. He can afford to run a game like this on the level, but it is not permitted in certain localities, being called a "game of chance"—in other words, a gambling device. A wheel run on percentage is a "percentage wheel."

Sloughing the Wheels

"Percentage wheels" always get a big play. Therefore, the operators try to run them everywhere. Sometimes they get away with it for a few days, then the authorities step in and call a halt. This is called "sloughing the wheels."

Flashers

Many of the old-style "percentage games" have been supplanted by electrical devices in which lights flash on and off. This attracts the crowd and gets a big play. These games are called "flashers." They are permitted in some localities where other "percentage games" are not.

Science and Skill

When the "percentage" games are barred operators resort to games of "science and skill." They put out big signs saying "Not a game of chance." The signs are correct for the player has no chance. These games are often permitted because they are not considered to be gambling devices. The player gets a reward because of the skill he exercises. But the "wise" authorities who "slough" the wheels and then let the games of "science and skill" go on are making a grave mistake. For in these games the operators use crooked methods that make it impossible for the players to win.

Gaff

A "gaff" is a secret device used in a carnival "joint," which makes it virtually impossible for the player to win. Nearly every game has its "gaff," which is sometimes called the "gimmick." When a game is made crooked it is said to be "gaffed." Now observe this: Some games are manufactured with a "gaff" already on them, but many games, especially those which are to be operated on a "percentage" basis, are perfectly fair when they come from the manufacturer. In fact, efforts are made to keep the "grifter" from "gaffing" the game after he gets it. But once a game is in the hands of an unscrupulous swindler he is free to do with it as he pleases. The regulation must be made when the game is played. No other legislation can produce results. There is no reason why carnival games should not be manufactured, because they do not have to be used for gambling purposes. The fault lies with the man who runs the game—not with the man who makes it.

Shills

"Shills" or "shillabers" are confederates of the "grifters" who run the crooked carnival games. They walk in with the crowd and win easily, so other persons take a chance. "Percentage" games are often fixed so that the "shill" wins. Stay around a carnival lot late at night and you will see the "shills" sneaking in the backs of tents, returning the prizes they have "won." These fellows walk around the midway carrying armloads of prizes and the suckers think the games are easy. In days of yore "shills" were called "cappers," but this term is unknown to many carnival men today.

Bloomers

A "bloomer" is a bad week—a time when the carnival lands in a "dead" town and no one will play the wheels or other games. Sometimes a carnival will hit a succession of "bloomers" and the operators will be out of luck. Their only hope is a big week or the country fairs late in the season when they hope to recoup their losses.

Red Ones

A big week is called a "red one." Sometimes a carnival will be out of luck for weeks at a time. Everybody will be broke and the going will be tough. Then the show hits a "red one" and the money pours in. Great stuff for the carnival men, but tough luck for the people of the town who pay up for the other places where folks were too wise to play the games.

Laydown

We come now to the game itself. Wherever players take chances on wheels or other games they put their money on numbered squares painted on the counter. This is called a "laydown." There is nothing crooked about it. It is just there to help the "suckers" spend their money.

Sucker

This means YOU if you play the carnival games. Enough said.

Various games are known under different names. These will be given in the pages that follow. Some games are known under two or three names. That makes no difference—they rake in the dough just the same.

Just a few words about the mental attitude of the carnival "grifter" and his outlook on life. He has his troubles the same as the rest of us. He has to watch his games and keep them looking on the square because every now and then a curious sheriff comes along and investigates.

The carnival owner is primarily a dispenser of amusements. He buys a ferris wheel, a merry-go-'round, a "whip" and other devices and comes to a city or a town to give the populace wholesome amusement.

But he seldom gets a guarantee that will pay him all expenses. He often works under the auspices of a local organization—otherwise he could not get into a town.

In order to make money he depends upon the game operators. He grants concessions to these people and they are given the dignified name of "concessionaries." They have to pay so much per week and a share of their profits. Thus they carry part of the burden and make it possible for the amusement-dispensing carnival proprietor to move his show from one town to another.

That fixes the owner all right and it helps out the local organization that signs up the carnival. But where does the concessionaire come in? He pays plenty and he won't go in the "racket" unless he thinks the carnival is going to meet with a lot of "red ones." He has to make enough during the season to pay for his ''joint,'' to pay for his privilege, to pay his own salary and that of his assistants and to make a good profit besides—generally enough to tide him over the winter months. Otherwise he would be in some less strenuous business. Now these people stay in the ''racket'' year after year. Some of them own a number of concessions. Where do they get their money? From the public. Even though they run games on a strict percentage basis they must be assured of an enormous profit or they will go broke.

What chance has the average person against an organized business like this? Very little. Look into the carnival game and study it, and the farther you go the more you will understand this.

The man who runs a carnival concession is not out to injure people; he would prefer to have a lot of suckers lose small amounts and come back to lose more than to have a few big saps lose their bank roll and then quit. He acts the part of a good fellow and his conscience never bothers him. He doesn't worry about the sucker. That isn't his business. Nevertheless, the ''grifters'' take in thousands of dollars every season. They are doing it all the time and they will probably continue. If the reader gets pleasure out of losing his money on the games at carnivals, let him go ahead. There is more thrill to it than throwing cash in the gutter, but the net result to the average player is just the same.

A fool and his money soon part on the carnival lot!

Spotting the Spot

The Easier It Looks the Harder It Is!

ANYONE who visits a fair where a ''spot the spot'' game is in operation will be immediately attracted by the simplicity and apparent fairness of the game. On a strip of oilcloth are painted half a dozen solid red circles each five inches in diameter. Beside each ''spot'' lie five loose discs of tin, each slightly more than three inches in diameter.

Having obtained a willing listener the operator picks up the five loose discs and, holding one a few inches above the large red spot, drops the disc so that it covers part of the spot. Then he drops another disc so that it partly overlaps the first one. He continues with the remaining discs, as shown in the large drawing. When he has dropped the last disc they have overlapped so neatly that not one speck of the red spot shows through. The spot has been completely covered.

''Try it,'' invites the operator. ''You must drop the discs—you can't place them in position or shove them after you've dropped them. Nothing but skill; just a little practice. Try it once for yourself. It won't cost you anything.''

The victim starts in. Time and again he tries to spot the elusive spot, lured on by an offer of ''three more tries for a quarter.'' But every time a vexatious bit of red peeps from among the neatly placed discs. The player studies the problem. If he possesses any mathematical knowledge he attempts a geometric solution. But every time, just as success seems certain, the last disc fails to cover the remaining space. Then the operator blandly gathers up the discs and, with apparent unconcern, lays them perfectly so that the last vestige of red is completely hidden.

The upper explanatory drawing shows how the discs should be laid to cover the spot. It illustrates the relative proportions of the discs and the spot. The spot is painted the required size and the discs are cut accordingly. Then everything is fair and the game depends, as it is supposed to, upon ''science and skill.''

But in laying the oilcloth upon the counter the cloth is stretched. Thus the circle of the ''spot'' is elongated. This simple action renders the game far more difficult of execution, for if the discs are properly placed, as shown in the lower explanatory diagram, a bit of red will show at the point of

---

Mitt Camps

ON the carnival lot a fortune-telling concession is called a ''mitt camp,'' because the gypsies who operate them are skillful palm readers. The proprietors of these establishments take in thousands of dollars every year and give nothing in return except a lot of useless misinformation. Traveling fortune tellers are good guessers who live by their wits and convince simple-minded people that they can tell their future. If some of them could tell their own futures, they would get the impression of a judge saying, ''Thirty days.''

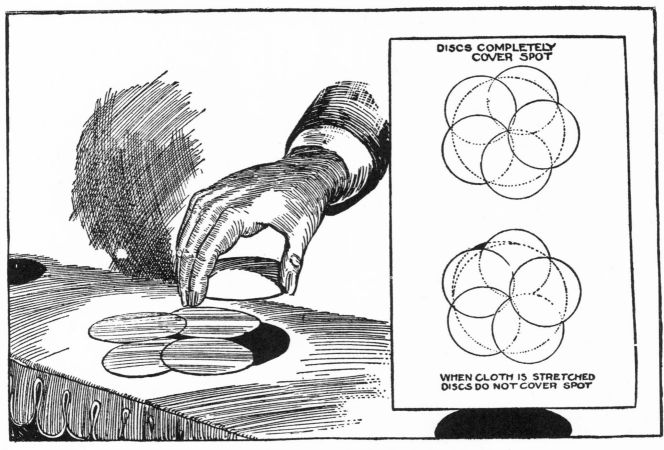

The operator can cover the spot every time, but the players never succeed.

elongation; and if that point is covered, the center will be laid open.

But even with the distorted circle it is still possible to "spot the spot," provided the operator places the first disc over the point of elongation. There is scarcely one chance in a hundred that the spectator will start correctly, and as the slightest deviation from the starting point will cause trouble the victim is doomed to failure and the operator cheerfully pockets the cash.

The Famous Silver Arrow

The Game That No One Can Detect — A Sure Winner for the Bunco Man

STEP this way, folks! Spin the arrow and win a prize! Nobody loses! Win a gold watch for a dime!"

The visitor at the carnival stops, looks and listens. Here is a game that certainly offers wonderful returns and great possibilities for a trifling expenditure. On a large counter are a number of bent nails, as shown in the large diagram. The nails are arranged in a circle so that they form a number of small sections. In the center on a nickel-plated stand is set a silver arrow or spindle. A strip of celluloid projecting downward from the point of the arrow impedes the arrow when it is spun and causes it to stop at one of the sections. At each section is a prize, and nearly one out of every four prizes is an article of value—a watch, a knife, a pipe, a cigarette case, or a razor.

Everything about the game appears so fair and above board that the visitor loses no time in starting to spin the arrow. But each spin brings him a small prize. Somehow the arrow never seems to stop at one of the valuable prizes and after losing all faith in the law of averages the player gives up in disgust and yields the arrow to some new player who feels certain that he can "beat the game."

The exact balance of the stand and arrow apparently prove that

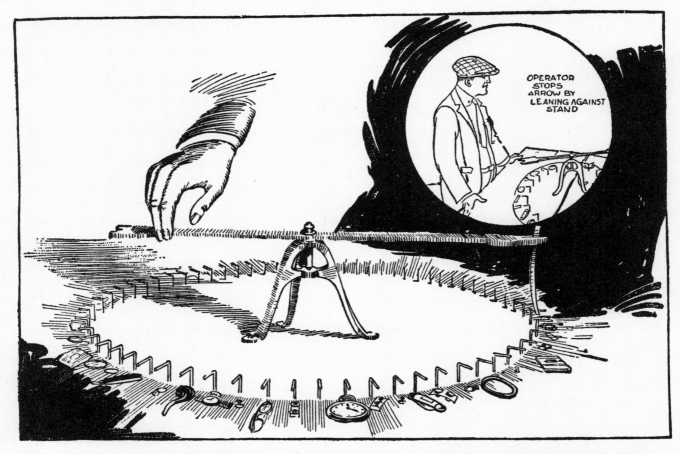

A twist of the wrist and the arrow speeds on its way. The player wins the prize at which it stops—but it passes all the big ones.

the device is fairly operated, but therein lies the fraud. If the stand is slightly tilted, the arrow will not spin freely, but the spindle, dragging against the sides of the hole in the stand, will retard the progress and the arrow will quickly come to a standstill if it is not spinning very rapidly.

The stand is perfectly balanced on the counter, but the counter itself, which is made up of three boards, may be tilted by leaning against it. Pressure applied to the rear of the counter causes the joints of the boards to press together and thus throw the metal stand slightly off balance. In this way the operator may, with no apparent effort, cause the arrow to slow down and stop.

The arrow is allowed to spin freely until it has nearly come to a standstill. At this point the operator leans against the counter (see small drawing). Just as the arrow is passing one of the large

prize sections he applies pressure to the counter and the arrow stops at one of the small prize sections. A skilled operator waits until the

last instant so that the way in which the arrow stops appears normal and excites no suspicion on the part of the players.

The Country Store Wheel

*Prizes for Everybody — But the Operator
Keeps the Big Ones*

"HERE y'are, folks! The country store! One dime wins a prize! Take your choice; everybody wins!"

A large revolving wheel, some four feet in diameter, laden with clocks, thermos bottles, kewpie dolls and other desirable articles, forms the center of attraction about which a large crowd is gathering. The wheel sets on a counter or stand, and is divided into a number of compartments. The large, central division contains a number of "capital" prizes, while the smaller "pockets" are filled with "inter-

mediate" prizes, valued at about twenty-five cents each, and "small" prizes, which are cheap articles, such as collar buttons, "put-and-take" tops, etc., which may be purchased at less than five cents each.

A player steps up to the wheel, pays a dime to the operator, and revolves the wheel by one of a number of knobs attached to the side. The whole wheel, prizes and all, spins round on the central pivot. The sight of the whirling wheel creates what the gamesters call a "flash," and attracts more customers.

As the wheel revolves the upright nails that protrude from the rim spin past a celluloid indicator (see illustration). When the wheel finally stops the indicator is resting in one of the sections formed by the upright nails, and thus the player discovers whether he has won a large, intermediate or small prize.

The "country store wheel" is, primarily, a fairly played game. As supplied by manufacturers, it is not "gaffed." The wheel is operated with a percentage in favor of the operator, although the odds seem to be greatly in favor of the player.

A glance at the top view of the wheel reveals an interesting fact. The central compartment, which contains the capital prizes, is the largest of all, and the casual observer would be impressed by that detail. But the large compartment is star-shaped, and the points are at the rim of the wheel, so there are only five single stopping points where a big prize may be won.

In the wheel illustrated below, the small prizes, which occupy very little space, have no less than 120 stopping points. On some wheels there are less small prize stops, but a larger number is necessary to give the operator a reasonable percentage.

The percentages then figure as follows: There are 140 stops. At ten cents a play, the operator receives $14. He gives out, if the averages run perfectly, capital prizes that cost him wholesale about $6. The fifteen intermediates run him approximately $2.50, while the 120 small prizes cost about the same figure. "Where, then," someone asks, "are the big profits made by the concession operators?"

The operator of the "country store wheel" is apt to ask himself that very question. If he is operating in certain localities he may be content with the profit of $3. But suppose that he is paying from $50 to $100 for the privilege of operating the game. He cannot afford to work at such a figure. Accordingly, he takes a pair of pliers and "gaffs" the game. The explanatory diagram shows how he does it.

At each capital prize stop he bends one nail slightly outward, and the next nail slightly inward. When the wheel is spun, the celluloid indicator first meets with the outward nail. It bends the indicator back at a sharp angle. If the wheel stops at that point, well and good; the indicator will be resting one section in front of the capital prize section. But suppose the wheel travels a fraction of an inch further on. The indicator snaps free of the outward nail with such force that it springs past the inward nail and comes to rest just one point beyond the capital prize section. Thus the operator never loses a large prize, and his output becomes less than $5 for every $14 taken in.

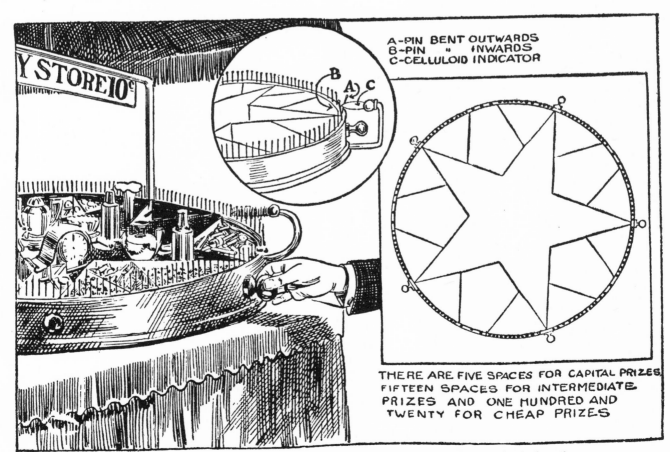

A—PIN BENT OUTWARDS
B—PIN " INWARDS
C—CELLULOID INDICATOR

THERE ARE FIVE SPACES FOR CAPITAL PRIZES, FIFTEEN SPACES FOR INTERMEDIATE PRIZES AND ONE HUNDRED AND TWENTY FOR CHEAP PRIZES

The country store wheel offers big returns for the dime invested—but its construction is deceptive.

The Devil's Bowling Alley

One of the Newest Attractions of the Midway— *A Carnival Game that Gets the Customers*

ONE of the most profitable and tempting of all the games seen at country fairs and carnivals is the "Devil's Bowling Alley," which appears as shown in the large drawing below.

Instead of a counter in front of the tent, there is a smooth, inclined board. A hundred wooden balls, each about three inches in diameter, are continually rolling down the "bowling alley." They drop through an opening at the lower end of the board, and roll back along another incline concealed beneath the counter. Then they are lifted by a mechanical contrivance operated by electricity, and again start their course down the alley.

Thus a perpetual stream of balls is rolling by, and the noise created, as well as the sight of the moving objects, combine to attract a large and curious crowd as soon as the machinery is set in operation, and the "joint" is opened for business. The operator picks up one of the balls as it rolls by, and shows that it contains a metal core. He takes a small metal rod and pushes out the core (see explanatory diagrams). A metal slip comes into view, and on it is seen a number. A peculiar feature of the numbers on the metal slips is that they are either between 10 and 20, or between 100 and 200.

The operator explains that the numbers between 10 and 20 win

the large prizes that are on exhibition, while the numbers between 100 and 200 gain a small "prize" of practically no value, such as a collar button or a toy. As the spectators watch the stream of rolling balls, the operator picks two or three at random, without even looking at them. He pushes out the core of each ball, and shows that every one he has taken contains a small number. He invites a spectator to pick one; and the result is the same. The operator points to the large prizes that would have been won had the spectator been "playing the game."

It does not take much persuasion to sell chances on the game at ten cents a ball, after the preliminary

The balls roll down the alley continuously. Anyone may carry a winning number, and the player seldom hesitates.

demonstration, and soon several persons are picking up the balls in hopes of obtaining prizes. But, strange to say, all of the balls they pick contain large numbers, and the operator's exhibition rack remains as nicely stocked as ever. The operator picks up another ball; he shows that it contains a small number, and thoughtlessly marks the ball with a crayon. A wily spectator seizes the marked ball as it comes by on the next round, but finds to his surprise that it contains a large number, and he realizes that he has been "sold."

The secret of the "Devil's Bowling Alley" is absurdedly simple, and is shown in the explanatory diagram. The trick lies in the metal slips contained in the wooden balls. All the balls contain high numbers, between 100 and 200. The space between the second and third figures is slightly greater than that between the first and second. Thus if the metal slip is pushed only two-thirds of the way out, it will appear as a small number; if pushed all the way out, it will appear as a large number.

The ball shown in the diagram is number 101. It can be shown either as number 101, or as number 10. Ball number 176 can be shown as either 176 or 17; ball number 135 can appear either as 135 or 13.

When the operator marks a ball, after showing it to be a small number, it does not matter if the spectator recognizes the marked ball and picks it up; for the operator can push the metal slip all the way out, and the spectator's "small number" has mysteriously changed to a large one!

Underneath the "bowling alley" the operator has ten extra balls concealed. These balls actually contain the small numbers from 10 to 20, and have some secret mark upon them so that the operator may recognize them. By releasing a catch beneath the counter, the real small-numbered balls may be released and allowed to mingle with the high-numbered ones. The operator keeps these balls in reserve in case someone detects the secret of the metal slips. The game is occasionally inspected by the authorities, and the operator is able to show a full quota of small-numbered balls by releasing the hidden store.

The Automatic Bowling Alley

A Game That Keeps its Own Score—It Looks Easy—But It Isn't

THIS is a game that appears to depend upon real science and skill. The player is provided with a number of wooden balls and he rolls them up an inclined alley in an effort to make them fall into numbered holes at the end of the alley.

Three wooden balls are used and the highest possible score is 75, gained by rolling all three balls into the single pocket marked 25. Every time a ball goes in the score is automatically registered on a dial.

Sometimes the player is offered a bigger prize for a score of 100 or 200. In this case he is provided with extra balls.

In the three-ball game scores of 60, 65, 70 and 75 win large prizes, the grand prize going to a score of 75. But the players seldom score as high as 60.

This is chiefly because of the difficulty of rolling the ball into a high pocket. The small numbered holes are in the way. In order to hit a high hole the player rolls the ball hard, hoping that it will reach the backboard and bounce into the 25 or the 20 holes.

But the backboard is a rubber cushion and it gives the ball so much impetus that it passes back over the high holes and falls into a low number.

It is, therefore, no easy matter to tally a high score on the automatic bowling alley unless the player tosses the balls directly into the high-numbered holes, but this is against the rules of the game.

By the use of a special "gaff" the bowling alley can be fixed so that no player can possibly score as high as 60 and this enables the operator to put up all sorts of attractive prizes.

Under the board is a movable device in the form of a sliding bar. This is shown as A in the explanatory diagram.

The lines B and C represent wires under the board. They are attached to the sliding bar at one end and to the opposite side of the board at the other.

The dotted lines show the positions of the wires when the bar A is pushed forward.

That enables the operator to drop balls into all the holes and to show that each ball is automatically registered when it is dropped in.

When the player is ready to roll the balls the operator slides the bar back and the thin wires come beneath the holes. If a ball starts to roll in any one of the three important pockets, it will bounce out again when it hits the wire.

The operator can offer the whole bowling alley and all the prizes as a reward to the man who shoots 60 or above, because such a high score is rendered impossible.

As a rule a game of this type is operated fairly because only a few large prizes are offered and the chances of winning them are very small. The rubber backboard takes care of most balls that might enter the high holes.

As manufactured, a game of this type is built squarely and will net its owner a fair profit if run on the square. The operator can "gaff" it for himself if he wishes.

Many carnival games are built fair by manufacturers, but still they are gambling devices, and it stands to reason that they are constructed to give the owner a big profit. Otherwise they could not be sold.

Every time a ball drops through an opening the dial registers the score.

The Three Marble Roll Down

Odd or Even Loses or Wins—By Use of a Simple Gaff, the Operator Has Complete Control

THE operation of the game is simplicity itself. Anyone viewing it in action soon understands it. A large frame, studded with nails, stands behind the counter. Above is a box with three compartments. At the bottom of the frame is a row of grooves, or "pockets," each one numbered, as shown in the illustration.

The operator drops three marbles in the top of the box; one marble in each compartment. Then he pulls a cord, opening trapdoors in the compartments, and the marbles roll down the frame.

When the marbles have reached the bottom and have settled in the "pockets," the operator adds up the numbers of the three "pockets" containing the marbles. If the total is even, the player is entitled to any of the "valuable" prizes on display; but if the total is odd, he is "out of luck," and is rewarded with a "small prize," such as a tin whistle, or some article of no intrinsic value.

The "gaff," or secret contrivance, is illustrated in the explanatory diagram. It costs the operator less than five cents and a few

The balls zig-zag down the frame—and the player waits expectantly for the prize he never gets.

minutes' work. Before opening his game, he takes the frame, and with a pair of pliers, bends the nails touched by the dotted lines illustrated in the diagram. The nails are quite close together, so that very slight bends, judiciously applied, make it impossible for a rolling marble to leave the broad "track" bounded by the dotted lines. The "track" widens toward the bottom, so that it leads directly into all of the odd numbered "pockets."

The beginning of the "track" starts at the right half of the center compartment. In the middle of that compartment, the operator inserts a glass push-pin. The result is obvious. If the marble is placed at the left of the push-pin it will keep to the left of the "track," and cannot possibly reach an odd numbered "pocket." It must terminate in one of the four even numbered "pockets" at the left of the frame. If, however, the marble is set to the right of the push-pin, it will follow the

Phoney Advertisements

THIS advertisement has caught plenty of suckers, as it is made to look like a real opportunity. Ads of this type are sometimes inserted in small journals where they get by before the publishers learn about them.

BUSINESS OPPORTUNITY

Be independent. Start a small business of your own. Big profits, small investment. All done by mail. We furnish instructions that have been used with big results. Full information regarding our new method. Send us only $1.00 for this authentic information.

KETCHEM AND CHEETEM
Itsyou, Io.

The unsuspecting victim gets just what he is promised. An explanation of how the grafters operate. They send him a copy of the ad, and names of papers and rates where it has been inserted. Then they tell him to insert the ad with his own name beneath it, print up a similar circular and send it to the suckers, just as they are doing!

"track," and come to rest in an even numbered "pocket."

The marbles that are placed in the two end compartments are sure to fall into even numbered "pockets" as they also are kept from entering the "track." In setting the marbles in the three compartments of the "Roll Down," the operator always takes care to put the center marble to the right of the push-pin. Thus the total of the three marbles will surely be odd, and the player loses. When the confederate plays the game, or the operator chooses to "throw away" a prize to stimulate business, he puts the marble to the left of the push-pin, and the three marbles come to rest in even numbered pockets, making an even total.

This game never fails to attract customers, because it seems as though they have an even chance of winning a large prize. If they thought twice they would realize that the operator could not afford to conduct his game upon such a generous basis.

The Game of Hoop Tossing
Most Everybody Falls for Its Tantalizing Fascination

THE drawing shows the "Hoop Tossing" game in operation. A large wooden platform is surrounded by a railing. On the platform are two or three dozen wooden blocks, each covered with velvet, or other cloth. On top of each block rests a prize of recognized value—a watch, a safety razor, a vase, or a vanity case. The player is provided with seven light, wooden hoops for the sum of ten cents. These he tosses at the wooden blocks and if he succeeds in "ringing" a block, the prize upon it becomes his property.

There is a tantalizing fascination about the game of "hoop tossing" that makes the player "come back for more" and the game proves a big money making proposition for the operator. It is hardly necessary to state that the player never wins, unless the operator wishes him to and the latter is rarely of a philanthropic turn of mind.

The operator, who is "in the game" to make all the money he can, is not content to rely on the law of averages. He resorts to a "gaff," or secret contrivance, which makes it impossible for the player to throw a "ringer."

The block upon which each prize rests is not a solid piece of wood, covered with velvet, as it appears to be. It is, in reality, made up of several layers of wood, as shown in the explanatory diagram. These layers are not firmly held together. They are quite loose, but are held in position by the velvet that covers them. When all of the layers of wood are flush and in proper alignment, the hoop will pass over the block quite easily. The operator demonstrates this fact by setting a hoop over the block, or even by lifting the block from the platform and passing the hoop over it. When he replaces the block on the platform, the operator by a simple, natural movement of his fingers, pushes the center layer of the block out of position. As the velvet covering is not over-tight, this operation is an easy matter. It serves to make the slide a trifle longer—just enough longer in fact to prevent the hoop from passing over the block. It then becomes impossible for any one to win a prize, no matter how skilled a tosser he may be. At any time, however, any hoop may be passed over any block, simply by pushing the layer back to its normal position.

Even though the player drops the hoop with utmost care he finds it almost impossible to ring a prize. Yet there are always new players willing to try.

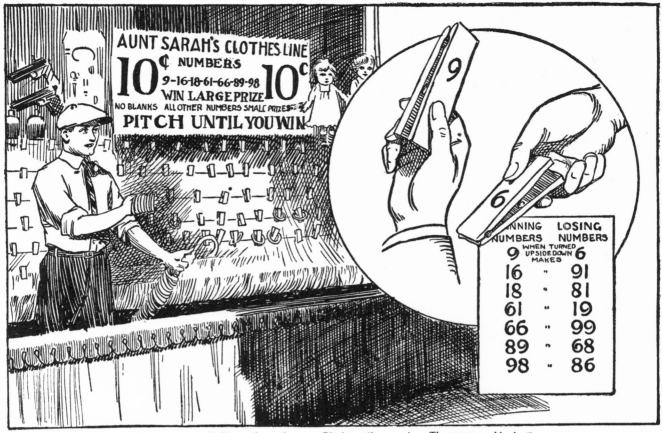

"Step right up, ladies and gentlemen. Pitch until you win. There are no blanks."

Aunt Sarah's Clothes Line

A Game That Makes Losers Out of Winners—It Looks Easy, But the Result is Always in the Hands of the Operators

NOBODY loses! Pitch until you win!" The visitor to the country fair stops in front of the small tent and gazes with interest at "Aunt Sarah's Clothes Line," where a group of young men are busily tossing wooden rings at wooden clothes-pins.

One of the players "rings" a clothes-pin. The operator removes it from the line, and turning it over, shows the number on the reverse. If it turns out to be one of the "big winners"—number 9, 16, 18, 61, 66, 89 or 98—the player receives a clock, a thermos bottle, a revolver or some other prize that is hanging on display. But if any other number is on the clothes-pin,

he is presented with a "small prize," such as a tin whistle, a pair of cardboard spectacles or a sachet bag.

The "Clothes Line" game depends upon a bold and barefaced swindle which, however, is rarely detected, and allows the player no redress.

The explanatory diagram shows the subtle principles of the game. Numbers 9, 16, 18, 61, 66, 89 and 98 can be instantly transformed into numbers 6, 91, 81, 19, 68 and 86, if the clothes-pins are held upside down! When the operator hangs the "winning" pins on the line, he holds them so that they appear to be the seven winning numbers. In hanging them with

the numbers away from the players, he turns the pins upside down, and thus the "winners" become "losers." When someone "rings" number 9, the operator takes the pin from the line, turns it around and exhibits it as number 6.

"Well, well," he says, smilingly. "Number six! That gives you a small prize." He reaches beneath the counter and brings out a tin whistle, which he gives to the unlucky player.

The explanatory diagram shows how the clothes-pin is held by the operator to disclose either a winning or losing number. The pins are reversible, so they may be hung either way.

The Famous Knife Rack

A POPULAR game that is seen on nearly every carnival "midway" is the "Knife Rack," illustrated above. It consists of a counter with a number of shelves in the background. A great many knives are set upright in the shelves, and the player is supplied with half a dozen wooden rings, upon payment of a dime. If he succeeds in "ringing" one of the knives, it becomes his property.

In front of the first row of knives a number of pegs are set upright. These pegs are quite similar to household carving irons. A revolver of recognized value hangs from each peg, and the player is informed that if he "rings" the peg, he wins the automatic. The knives are soon forgotten and the player tosses ring after ring in hopes of winning one of the coveted firearms. But, needless to say, his efforts are unsuccessful, and after squandering several dollars he quits in disappointment.

The knife rack is "gaffed" very simply but very cleverly. The explanatory diagram reveals the secret of the player's unsuccessful efforts.

The knob at the top of the carving iron has a backward direction, as shown in the diagram—a peculiarity found on nearly every carving iron in household use. As a matter of fact, the operators can use ordinary carving irons if they so desire, although the "pegs" are generally made especially for the knife racks.

Figure "A" in the diagram shows how smoothly a ring may be slipped over the knob of the peg, from the proper direction. Figure "B," however, illustrates the impossibility of "ringing" the peg from the wrong direction. There is not a chance in the world of slipping the ring in Figure "B" over the knob.

When the game is in operation the tip of the knob (side "A") is turned away from the player. The peg then appears as shown in figure "C." No wonder it looks easy! But it is a physical impossibility for the player to "ring" the peg while the knob is turned away from him.

Of course the operator can, at any time, demonstrate the "fairness" of the game by dropping on a ring from the rear. If he wishes to throw a few on for himself, he previously turns the tip of the knob toward the front. Even then it takes some skill to toss on a ring, but the operator is closer to the peg than is the player. When he has succeeded in "ringing" a few he takes the rings off the peg, and at the same time turns

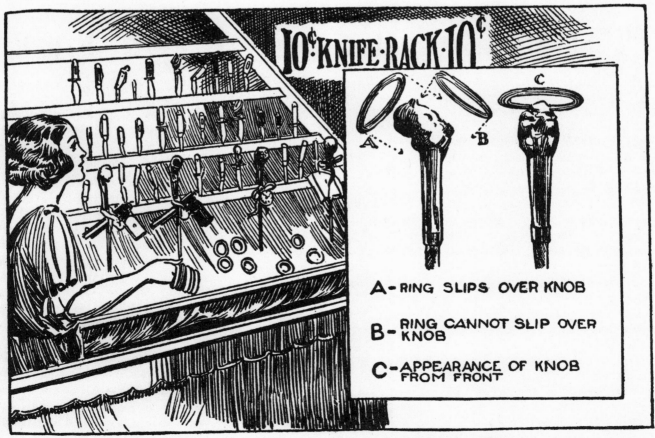

A - RING SLIPS OVER KNOB

B - RING CANNOT SLIP OVER KNOB

C - APPEARANCE OF KNOB FROM FRONT

You can toss a hundred rings at the knife rack, and never win a prize.

WIRE TO FRONT OF STAND. WHEN OPERATOR PULLS THIS WIRE CATS MAY BE REMOVED WHEN WIRE IS SLACK SPRING PULLS BAR BACK

ARMS ON BARS ACT AS PINS FOR HINGES

SPRING

The cat rack does a big business. The targets are easy to hit, but hard to knock off.

The Game of Cats on the Rack

HIT the babies! Knock 'em off and win a prize! Step this way, boys!" A row of four solemn, painted cats sit invitingly at the end of an alley, and for the small sum of ten cents one has the privilege of projecting three baseballs at the dummy figures.

If, in three attempts, he succeeds in "knocking off" one cat, he receives a cigar of questionable quality as a reward. For two cats, two cigars; while for three cats— a perfect score—a prize of real value is at stake.

The "cat-rack" invariably does a big business. The targets are large, and easy to hit; but they are heavy, and it is difficult to knock them clear of the rack. Often they will fall over, but will not fall off and the cat must be knocked completely off to count in the player's favor. A casual spectator, who

happens to notice the game carefully, will be surprised to observe how often a player will successfully "kill" two of the cats, and then fail to knock the third clear of the rack.

The "gaffing" of a game of this sort seems a difficult problem. All of the cats must be free at the beginning of the game. If the player misses his first or second throw there is no need to use the "gaff," as there is no danger of three cats being knocked from the rack.

Each cat is backed by a heavy piece of wood, at the bottom of which is a hinge. Behind the cats is a metal rod, with four projecting rods, each of which fits into the open posts of the four hinges. At one end of the rod is a strong spring, which pulls the projecting rods into place. At the other end is a strong wire (not illustrated).

This wire runs out at the side of the rack and into the railing that surrounds the alley. (See the large drawing.) The wire runs through the rail and terminates beneath the counter, where it may be quickly reached by the operator.

Before starting the game the operator secretly slips her hand under the counter and pulls the wire, hooking the end of it over a nail. This extends the spring and pulls the small projecting rods out of the hinges. As soon as a player has knocked two cats off the rack the operator reaches under the counter and releases the end of the wire. The spring snaps back, and pulls the rods into the hinges of the two cats that remain. Those cats may now be knocked over, but they will turn on the hinge and will not be able to fall from the rack.

The Tilting Roly-Poly Board

An Automatic Winner That Fools the Players—
A Type of Game Seen at Every Carnival

THE bunco games seen at fairs and carnivals are of two types: Games of chance and games of "science and skill." As the previous articles of this series have shown, the games of chance are usually operated on a "percentage" basis, the operator making a definite profit every time the game is played; whereas the games of "science and skill" are apparently greatly in favor of the player, but, thanks to a "gaff" or secret contrivance, the operator makes the player's chances negligible.

There is another class of game that is a sort of hybrid or composite of the games of chance and "science and skill." To the player it appears to be a game of chance, but with very good odds in his favor. Nevertheless, the game possesses all the deceptive allurements of the games of "science and skill." It looks easy, but is not. A typical game of this sort is "Roly-Poly." The large illustration shows it in operation.

The player lays a dime on the counter in front of a tilting board that is studded with nails and is divided at one end into eight pockets. By tilting the contrivance up and down, as shown in the upper explanatory diagram, six marbles are made to roll from one end to the other. At the outset of the game the marbles are at the end where the name "Roly-Poly" appears. The player tips the board so that the marbles roll down among the nails, following a haphazard course.

When they reach the bottom the operator counts up the numbers of the pockets in which they lie. For example, the pockets are numbered 3, 5, 4, 1, 6, 3, 2, 4. The marbles roll, let us suppose, as follows: two into Pocket 3 (at the left); two into Pocket 5; one into Pocket 6; one into Pocket 2. The operator counts up: "3 and 3 are 6; 5 and 5 are 10, making 16, and 6 is 22 and 2 makes 24." The player's total is 24.

The game is fascinating; and it looks easy; but the odds are hopelessly against the player.

It will be readily seen that there are thirty possible totals. The lowest possible score is 6; the highest 36. In order to score six, all of the balls must roll into Pocket 1; to score thirty-six, all must roll into Pocket 6. The chart of prizes shows that totals of 6, 7, 8, 9, 10, 11 and 31, 32, 33, 34, 35, 36 win valuable prizes. In other words, there are twelve possible totals out of thirty-six that are "winners," and the three lowest and three highest numbers carry prizes of exceptional value. The unsophisticated player thinks that he has a fine chance of winning, but if he studied the game from a mathematical standpoint he would be surprized how greatly his chances would dwindle. And if he studied the mechanical construction of the game he would also learn that, although the game contains no "gaff" or concealed mechanism, it is a practical impossibility for him to score 6, 7, 8 or 34, 35, 36. In fact, the operator could safely offer the town hall or the first national bank as prizes to the player attaining one of those scores.

A study of the explanatory diagram will make matters clear. It will be noticed that the spikes are so set that diagonal channels are formed. Start from the center of the board at the top and follow the arrows. They indicate the directions of the channels. The balls, coming against the first nails, are thrown toward the sides of the board and are kept away from the 1 and 6 pockets. And those are the pockets that must be filled in order to win a prize!

"But," someone asks, "don't the players become suspicious when they see the marbles roll to the sides each time?"

The answer is quite simple. All of the marbles do not roll to the sides. In their downward course they collide with one another, and one or two of the balls are thrown into an inward channel. Accordingly, almost every time the board is tilted there will be one or two marbles that will roll into the one pocket or the six pocket, but never enough to total a winning score. If two marbles collide in such a manner that one will be diverted into a channel leading to Pocket 1, the other will be thrown in the opposite direction and will terminate in a higher numbered pocket.

By way of a test, the author has experimented with one of these devices and has kept tabulation of the scores registered. In 100 rolls the highest score made was 28, the lowest 16. On more than seventy occasions one or more marbles entered Pockets 1 and 6, but never more than three.

Several other games are worked on this order. They are intended for a ten-cent "play" and are called "grind stores" by the "profession." Wherever there is a big crowd the operator of one of these games will make big profits, for many players will "take a chance" and the operator's supply of prizes will not diminish.

"Honest John" or "The Drop Case"

THE "bunco man" who plies his trade in "closed territory," where the laws are not favorable to gambling devices, cannot afford to carry elaborate games which may be seized by the authorities. He prefers to operate a small, quick-working contrivance, which will net him big profits and permit him to make a quick departure.

The "Drop Case" is a great favorite with swindlers of this type. It is made up to appear as a dress suit case (see large illustration), and the man who carries it appears to be an ordinary traveler. But when he has found a suitable spot at the fair grounds he becomes the extraordinary gamester. He sets his suitcase on a counter, or on the step of his automobile, opens it, and reveals to the public a portable Monte Carlo that brings joy to every would-be gambler in the vicinity.

The inside of the cover of the "suitcase" has a complete list of the prizes painted on it. The customer is provided with a marble, which he is at liberty to drop in one of three holes at the top of the case. The marble drops from nail to nail behind a sheet of glass and finally comes to rest in a pocket at the bottom of the case. On a metal strip, which extends across the case, a little over an inch from the bottom, the numbers of the respective pockets are painted, so that the player can tell at a glance whether he wins or loses.

The operator drops a marble into one of the holes. It rolls down and into a winning pocket. Then he lifts a little door at the end of the case (see "end view" in the explanatory drawing), and the marble rolls out. The operator does not touch the case; he even lets the player lift the little door to release the marble. Then the player pays a dime (or more often a quarter), and drops in the marble himself.

Each player who tries the "Drop Case" loses, despite the apparent fairness of the game, unless a confederate of the operator happens to be in the crowd, as is often the case. The confederate wins at last and when the customers begin to wane or when the "bunco man" suspects the proximity of a sheriff the game is closed. The gamester shuts the suitcase and walks away through the crowd, philosophizing on the gullibility of the human race, and mentally counting up the day's profits.

The "Drop Case" is intended as a quick money-maker, and for this reason it invariably contains a "gaff"—a secret contrivance which enables the operator to control the falling marble and prevent it from falling into a winning pocket.

The "gaff" consists of a narrow metal rod which is hidden from view by the metal strip on which the numbers of the different pockets are painted. It will be noticed in the large illustration that the numbers of the pockets are alternately winning and losing, the even pockets "winners," the odd ones "losers."

The hidden metal rod contains a number of projecting studs which extend almost to the glass. These studs are arranged in pairs, and each pair guards a "winning poc-

ket." The hidden rod, however, can be pushed across about an inch. This action places the various studs over the tops of the losing pockets, so that the marble will roll into a "winner." In other words, the game may be "set" to win or to lose.

Under the imitation leather covering at one end of the case is a concealed button, similar to the button which opens a folding camera. When the operator pushes this button the rod is shoved inward so that the studs cover the losing pockets. Then he drops a ball into the case and it quite naturally falls into a winning pocket. Now comes the ingenious part of the device. When the little door at the end of the case is opened to release the marble a hidden catch is also lifted, which, through the aid of a concealed spring, releases the "gaff." The hidden rod slides back into its original posi-

tion, pushing out the concealed button.

In brief the "gaff" is automatically set against the player and the winning pockets are guarded by the studs on the hidden rods. Every time a marble is dropped in it falls into a losing pocket and the players lose time after time. When the operator's confederate arrives on the scene the operator slyly pushes the concealed button and the "shill" (confederate) wins on his first attempt. As soon as the marble rolls out of the little door a player hastily seizes it and drops it in, but the "gaff" has already been released and the player pays over another quarter.

Often the operator offers large money prizes to any winners and charges a dollar for each play. In this way he wins large sums in a very few minutes—and makes a quick "getaway" in his automobile.

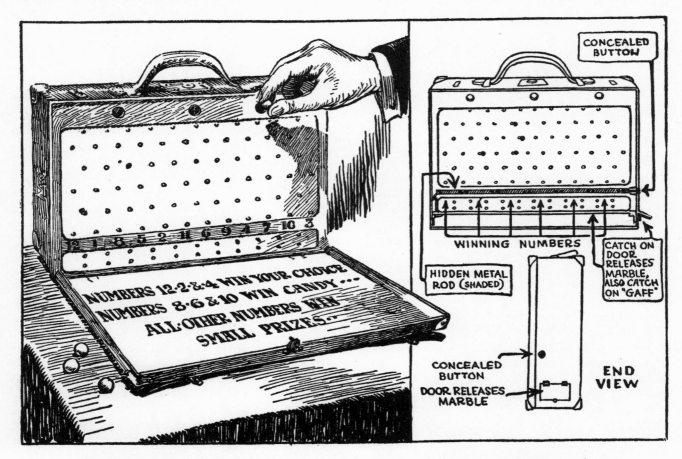

What appears to be a suit-case is a mechanical gambling contrivance that nets its owner heavy earnings.

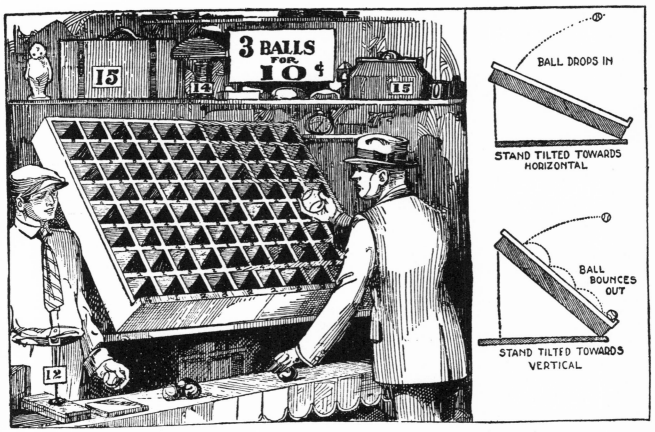

The longer the player tosses at the baseball rack the less he realizes how much he is paying.

The Deceptive Baseball Rack

DROP 'em in the squares, boys; you can't miss! All you need is a good eye and a little practice! Three balls for a dime!" This is the cry of the bunco man who operates the baseball rack—a game of the "science-and-skill" type that has recently come into great popularity.

The man who stops long enough to take an interest in this alluring game is almost certain to "take a chance" on it and risk a few dimes. The longer he tosses, the nearer he comes to his objective and the less he realizes how much he is paying, until he finds himself two or three dollars short and without the coveted prize for which he had been tossing.

The game is quite simple. An inclined rack is honeycombed with a number of square wooden pockets

which vary in number according to the size of the rack. The rack in the illustration contains eighty pockets.

The following table shows the arrangement of the numbers below the various pockets:

Top row:	5 5 5 5 5 5 5 5 5 5
	5 3 5 2 4 5 3 5 1 4
	3 2 4 1 5 4 3 4 5 3
	4 1 2 4 3 3 4 2 1 4
	3 1 4 2 3 2 4 3 1 4
	1 2 4 2 1 3 1 2 4 3
	2 1 3 1 2 4 2 1 3 4
Bottom row:	1 1 2 3 2 2 1 3 2 1

The player tosses three baseballs. These balls have a marked tendency to "pop out" of the pockets and bounce down to the bottom of the rack; but they cannot bounce completely off, due to the high ledge at the bottom. In other words, any ball that misses

the pocket for which it is tossed is bound to terminate on the bottom row, so that it will never be a "blank."

After the player has tossed three balls the numbers of the pockets in which the balls rest are added up. The lowest possible score is 3; the highest is 15. To win the player must score 12, 13 or 15. To score 12 he must make 4-4-4, 5-4-3 or 5-5-2; to score 13 he must make 5-4-4 or 5-5-3; 14 requires 5-5-4; 15 needs 5-5-5.

There are two numbers which stand out as essentials in order to win a prize. They are 4 and 5. To win the smallest prize, which is a good-sized box of candy (for a score of 12), the player must toss two of those essential numbers. And that is where the fun begins —for the operator!

The player finds that, time after time, his best-aimed efforts will result in the ball jumping out of the desired pocket and bounding down to the bottom row. And on the bottom row the numbers 4 and 5 do not appear. The board is tilted forward at such an angle that only one throw in ten will result in the ball staying in the hole into which it is tossed. The player has two pitfalls. First, ball after ball will bounce down to the bottom row and injure his score; second, if he does make the peculiar type of shot that will stay in the pocket, he is likely to miss one of the essential pockets, and undergo the chagrin of seeing his ball nestling comfortably in a 1, 2 or 3 situated on one of the higher rows.

The explanatory diagram shows how the game may be adjusted by the operator. The board is set on metal uprights, which are arranged so that the rack may be held at any angle from the horizontal to the vertical. Naturally, if the board is nearly horizontal, the balls will stay where they are tossed; if it is nearly vertical, they will jump out and bounce to the bottom.

The operator experiments before the crowd has arrived and sets the board at just the most tantalizing angle—one that will permit the ball to stay in, almost, but not quite. Then he is ready for business. It is next to impossible for any one to score a 14 or a 15, and so win one of the big prizes, and very few 12 and 13 prizes will pass across the counter.

Sometimes the operator will begin the week with a lot of cheap but "flashy" prizes. He will set the rack well toward the horizontal, and will "throw away" many of the prizes. But as the big Saturday business approaches he puts up large prizes, and shifts his rack to an impossible range. His store, or "joint," has been well advertised by his winning customers, for the plaster has not yet begun to fall off the "handsome pieces of statuary" which they have won.

The Shell Game

*Otherwise Known as Thimble Rig—an Old, Old Swindle
That Is Ever New—One of the Most
Famous of Bunco Games*

OF all the "bunco games" and swindling systems, the "shell game" is the most notorious. It has appeared in many places under many names, such as "thimble rig," "walnut shell and pea," and others. But the game is the same wherever it is played. It is the surest and simplest method ever devised to take away a man's money.

"The walnut shell and pea" is the most descriptive title for the "shell game," for it names the primitive objects which are utilized in the game. A pea and three walnut half shells are all that the bunco man requires. With these, and his bold dexterity, he reaps a bigger harvest than the operators of elaborate wheels and flashy "joints."

The bunco man who works the "shell game" plies his trade in an obscure corner of the fair grounds, where the authorities are not apt to be. Sometimes he is more bold and works in between two of the concession tents. Or he may be the operator of a permitted game, and when he sees an opportunity introduces the "thimble rig." In some localities he can run his graft unmolested. But in any event he can quickly hide or dispose of his entire apparatus—the pea and three shells—the moment he is warned by his trusty "shillaber" —his confederate who stands in the background.

Just as in "three-card monte," the game with which the "shell game" is so often associated, the bunco man depends upon his "shills" to bring him customers. But the task in this case is a much easier one and the "shill"—often there is only one—plays a comparatively inactive part in the swindle.

The brief visit of the wise" young man who comes to the fair ground with a bulging wallet and a swelled head will tell the story of the "shell game."

This enterprising individual risks a few quarter dollars on a "wheel" and when he loses turns away in disdain. At the same time another man also turns away and casually walks along beside him.

"The old fair's kinda dead this year," grunts the newcomer.

"Sure is," replies our hero. "I'd like to see a regular game worth playing."

"You won't see many of 'em here," says the stranger. "I've been all over the grounds and haven't found one yet.

The conversation once begun, both recall the many "real" fairs they have seen. The "wise" man, in particular, begins to boast of the money that he has "knocked off."

Suddenly the stranger who, needless to say, is the "shill," holds out his hand.

"Take a look at this!" he exclaims.

He and his victim stop between two tents and there witness the "shell game" in operation.

The operator lays a pea on the table. Over it he sets one of the three walnut shells. Then he pushes the three shells around the little table, as though to confuse the spectator. (See large drawing.)

"Who has a dollar on it?" he calls.

The "shill" pulls a dollar from his pocket and throws it on the table, pointing at one of the shells. The operator lifts it, reveals the pea, and grudgingly pays a dollar to the "shill."

"This is soft!" thinks the victim. "It may fool the rubes, but here is where I make some cash!"

The pea is once more covered. This time both the "shill" and the victim win a dollar. The operator looks worried. Again he covers the pea and mixes shells more than before.

"How about some real money?" says the victim. He lays down a $10 bill and pushes the "shill" aside. "Ten dollars on the middle shell!"

"You're on," replies the operator. "Pick up the shell."

The victim does so, and, to his surprise, finds no pea beneath it. Then the operator blandly lifts one of the other shells, revealing the pea. The rout has then begun. The victim tries to regain his $10, but he always picks the wrong shell. He tries guesswork; he picks a shell which he thinks is not covering the pea, in an attempt to "double-cross" the operator. But even then

he is wrong. The pea is always under some other shell. At last, "broke" and discouraged, he is forced to retire in favor of some new victim.

The explanation of the elusive pea is quite simple. A reference to the explanatory diagrams shows how the swindle is accomplished. The "pea" is not real, but is an imitation, made of rubber. When the operator sets a walnut shell over it he really sets the edge of the shell on the rubber "pea." (See Figure 1.) By pressing on the shell the "pea" is flattened and the shell does not tilt up.

The next movement is to push the shell forward. The operator does this with his right hand while he pushes another shell forward with his left. The result is that the little rubber ball pops out at the back of the shell. (See Figure 2.) With a deft movement of his little finger the operator secretly catches

the "pea" and steals it away. (See Figure 3.)

A man experienced at the "shell game" can perform this movement to perfection, without the slightest chance of detection. Of course, the victim is bound to lose; for whichever shell he picks is sure to be empty. Then the operator picks up one of the other shells and by a deft reversal of his previous movements introduces the "pea" under the unchosen shell.

The victim loses his money and the stage is all set for a repetition of the swindle.

During winter months operators of the "shell game" hibernate in large cities and pick up suckers at leisure. They station themselves in small alleys and wait for their confederates to bring in players. Someone keeps watch while the game is in progress. The moment the victim has lost his roll the gang scatters. When the police arrive no one is there.

1 RUBBER PEA
EDGE OF SHELL IS PRESSED ON PEA

2
SHELL IS PUSHED FORWARD

3
PEA IS STOLEN BY LITTLE FINGER

Three shells and a pea constitute the bunco man's equipment. With these simple objects he completely deceives the players, and never fails to win. You can't find the pea for it isn't there!

It is easy to roll the balls down the ladder, but difficult to make them stop!

The Hurdle Ladder

ROLL 'em down the ladder, boys! Everybody wins! Try your turn on the ladder!" This is the cry of the bunco man who operates the "hurdle ladder" and it invariably attracts a crowd of interested spectators, who, in turn, become enthusiastic players.

The game is simplicity itself, and it looks just hard enough to be genuine and just easy enough to tempt the player into rolling the ball down the ladder, which is depicted in the large illustration. A wooden ball is rolled down the incline and jumps from rung to rung until it finally comes to rest. Each section is numbered and the player receives a prize according to the value of the section whereon his ball rests.

Three or four of the sections, which are designated on a large chart (see illustration), pay "large prizes"—articles of recognized value. All the other sections pay "small prizes" which are worth considerably less than the dime the player spends.

The lack of success experienced by those who play the "hurdle ladder" is due to a peculiarity in the construction of certain rungs of the ladder. The explanatory diagrams show where the deception lies. It is obvious that if the player is to win, his ball must come to rest on one of the rungs that forms the furthermost boundary of one of the winning sections. These rungs may be termed the "winning rungs." In order to keep the ball from stopping on a "winning rung" the operator has those rungs made with one side shaved down so that it is almost flat instead of being rounded as are the normal rungs. Only one side of each "winning rung" is flattened, for a reason which will be explained later.

The shaved side of each "winning rung" is uppermost, but its flatness cannot be noticed, due to the peculiar painting of the rung which is sometimes a jet black, but more often a series of lengthwise stripes. Thus the rungs are literally "camouflaged," so that they appear to be quite round.

When the ball rolls down the incline it bounces from rung to rung. When it bounces onto one of the "winning rungs" the flat side of the rung is unable to withhold it and the ball slides over into the next section where it stops on a "losing rung." Thus the player can never win.

The "hurdle ladders" have the "winning rungs" slightly loose, so that they can be turned round side up, as shown in the left explanatory diagram. In this case the ball will stop on one of the "winning rungs" if it is rolled cleverly.

Carnival Roulette

THE carnival roulette wheel differs considerably from the famous game after which it is patterned for reasons which will appear later. Instead of consisting of a single wheel which revolves, it has two wheels, one set over the other, as depicted in the large drawing. Both of these wheels have a center rod which runs up through them and is tightened by a set-screw at the top.

The upper wheel, which is a saucer-like contrivance, revolves freely. Near its center are three small holes each large enough to allow the passage of a little black ball. The top wheel is revolved and the ball is dropped upon it. After whirling about for some time and trying vainly to climb over the side of the wheel the ball drops through one of the central holes and falls on to the lower wheel, where it rolls into one of the numbered pockets.

If the ball rolls into an odd numbered pocket, all the players are entitled to prizes worth from fifty cents to a dollar. If, however, it rolls into an even numbered pocket, nobody wins.

The secret lies in the set-screw which tightens the rod that runs through the centers of the two wheel (Fig. 1). The operator occasionally tightens or loosens this screw so as to allow the upper wheel the proper freedom of revolution. But the screw, by a unique mechanical arrangement, also controls an inner rod, or level, which is inside the center rod. This lever extends beneath the lower wheel and has sixteen arms that run off at right angles. Each of these arms terminates an inch or two in front of the sixteen odd numbered pockets and on the end of each arm is an upright needle point.

The result is this: When the screw is tightened the needle points are raised and either protrude through the cloth or, more often, raise the cloth very slightly (the points in this case being blunt). Naturally, when the ball rolls toward an odd pocket it encounters the tiny projection which efficiently deviates it from its course and causes it to roll into an even numbered pocket (Fig. 2). By merely loosening the screw the operator can make the game work "on the square" and can thus demonstrate the fact that it is quite possible for the ball to roll into a "winning" pocket.

In carnival roulette the player experiences the thrill of Monte Carlo, but the odds are all against him.

BALL MUST MISS PIN ON OUTWARD SWING & STRIKE IT COMING BACK

Operator Shifts Frame So Ball Will miss Pin.

Knocking over the cone seems like child's play, but those who try it are due for a surprise.

The Cone and Base Ball Swindle

THE "ball and cone" is a recent development of the "swinging ball." The ten-pin is replaced by a wooden cone, which stands on a piece of oilcloth. The cloth is marked with a circle to indicate the spot where the cone must stand. Instead of the heavy bowling ball a baseball is used. It dangles from the end of a string and hangs alongside the wooden cone.

The cone is stood on the circle and the player is allowed to push the ball past the right side of the cone. The ball swings over the counter and if, on its swing back, it strikes the cone and knocks it over the player receives a grand prize for his successful strike. If the ball misses the cone, he loses his money. The operator first demonstrates the game and, as he handles the ball very artfully, he succeeds in knocking over the cone on

his first or second attempt. The player, believing that he can master the game himself, is quite willing to try his luck. But every time he swings the baseball it misses the cone by at least an inch.

The "gaff" that controls the "ball and cone" is not in the cone nor in the counter upon which it stands. The trick lies in the framework from which the baseball hangs—a simple crossbar set upon two upright posts. It is obvious that, if the ball is to be swung from the right of the cone, the upper end of the string must be directly above or a trifle to the right of the cone in order that the ball may strike the cone on the reverse swing. Such is the actual arrangement. The ball must be pushed almost straight forward on its outward course. If it is given a slight spin to the right, it will almost

tainly hit the cone on its return journey.

The framework, however, is slightly loose. In its normal position it is fair and square. But if the operator leans against one of the upright posts and pushes toward the player's left, the crossbar will be shifted to the left. When the ball is swung from the right it is bound to miss the cone, no matter how cleverly it may be swung, for the return swing must be to the left of the top of the string and, therefore, to the left of the cone.

When the player is ready the operator leans forward to set up the cone on its spot. As he does so he rests his hand on the upright post and shifts it to the left. No wonder the player loses! By pushing back the post the apparatus is again set properly so that the cone may be knocked over.

The Cigarette Shooting Gallery

THE "Cigarette Shooting Gallery," a carnival game of fairly recent invention, has attained remarkable popularity, and is now seen on virtually every "midway." It is a game that appeals to every man who sees it and, accordingly, is a good money-maker for its owner. It is clearly a game of "science and skill," a fact that permits it being run almost anywhere.

Behind the counter of the "shooting gallery" are a number of glass stands arranged on shelves or "steps." On each stand is a pack of cigarettes. The packs range in value from seven cents to thirty. The player is supplied with an air rifle and three corks, which he loads in the muzzle of the gun. He pays ten cents for the privilege, and then blazes away at the packages of cigarettes. Any pack that he knocks off its glass stand is given to him as a reward for his marksmanship.

The peculiar appeal of the "shooting gallery" lies in the fact that the player is actually getting some pleasure from playing it, even if he wins nothing. For this reason it is unfair to place the game in the same category with the numerous swindle devices which are operated for the express purpose of taking in the "suckers." The "cigarette shooting gallery" is, in one respect, an amusement device, and many persons patronize it with no special interest in winning a prize. The very fact that none of the cigarette packs are worth more than thirty cents apiece keeps away the man who is out to make a "big winning."

The explanatory diagram shows why the player who goes after the big packs usually fails to win. A large package of cigarettes is quite heavy in comparison with the light corks used in the air rifles. If a pack is hit squarely with a well-directed shot, the pack will fall over, but if it is set well forward on the glass stand, it will not fall off the stand. The pack falls backward, as though on a hinge, but there is not enough force in the shot to knock it off the stand.

A method whereby a player may win is one that forms a source of annoyance to the operator, and makes him keep on the alert all the time. When the player loads his gun he pushes a large headed thumtack into the end of the cork. This considerably increases the weight of the cork and renders it quite capable of knocking a large pack of cigarettes off the glass stand. The operator is usually quick to detect this deception on the part of the player, as he looks carefully at each cork which has knocked off a pack of cigarettes.

The player pays ten cents and blazes away at the cigarette packs, using corks as ammunition for his pop-gun.

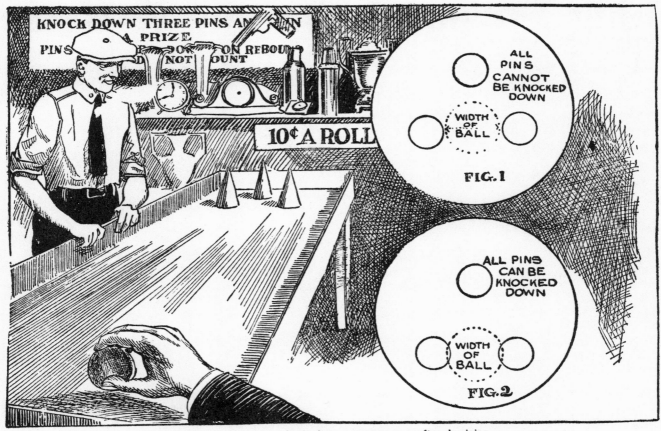

It appears to be very simple, but appearances are often deceiving.

The Famous Three Pin Game

THE simplicity of the game appeals to every one. Three pins are set up as shown in the large illustration. The player rolls a wooden ball and, if he knocks over the three pins, wins a prize. He is allowed one roll which costs him ten cents. The operator obligingly shows how easily it can be done and then sets up the pins for the player. The pins must be knocked over on the roll; rebounds from the backboard do not count.

To the player who knows anything of bowling, the "Three Pin Game" seems extremely simple. In bowling, it is not an uncommon feat for a player to knock over all ten pins with one roll and in the "Three Pin Game" he has only to "strike" three pins in order to win a dollar for his dime. But somehow or other his efforts are unsuccessful. He has no difficulty in knocking down two of the pins, but the third invariably stands untouched.

The explanatory diagrams give the game away. When the operator sets up the pins he places them according to tiny marks on the board. The pins are set so that the two front ones are on a line. They are just so far apart that the ball will pass between them, if it is aimed directly at the rear pin.

What is the result? A perfectly placed roll will miss the front pins entirely, and only strike the rear pin. If the player's roll deviates to either side, as it invariably does, it will knock over one of the front pins, and continuing onward, will take away the rear pin. But it is a physical impossibility to knock over both front pins.

In bowling the triangle of ten pins is set up with the "king pin" in front. If the "king pin" is struck squarely the heavy ball will crash into the solid mass of pins and scatter them right and left. But in the "Three Pin Game" the "king pin" is at the rear. The ball and the pins are made from light wood, and there is no rebound of the ball. A pin will not fall unless it is struck by the ball, and since the ball can hit only two of the pins, it is a hopeless task to knock over all three.

When the operator "demonstrates" the game, or when one of his confederates approaches the counter he sets up the pins about an inch closer together. When they are in this position, a well-placed shot directed at the rear pin will cleanly bowl over the two front pins, as shown in the lower diagram. One pin will be knocked to the left, the other to the right, and the ball, continuing on, will take away the rear pin also.

Ring a Watch and Take It Home

THE game is simplicity in itself; no complicated rules disturb its operation. A number of wooden stands, of a keystone shape, are set on a series of "steps" or racks a few feet behind the counter of the "joint." There is a watch on every wooden stand. The player is given three wooden hoops for ten cents. He is allowed to toss the hoops, and if he "rings" one of the stands, the watch resting on that stand becomes his property.

The most interesting feature of the "Watch La" game is the fact that it is almost impossible for the player to win one of the watches. The slant of the top of each stand is so great that a hoop cannot lodge over the stand. If the inside of the hoop strikes the lower edge first, it will drop down too quickly for the far side of the hoop to go over the point of the keystone. A similar situation arises if the hoop first strikes the point.

If the hoop is tossed high in the air, so that it comes down squarely over the stand, success may be realized, but only a superhuman tosser could control such a throw.

How, then, are the victims induced to try the game? Common sense should cause them to demand a demonstration to prove that the ring tossing feat could actually be accomplished. This the operator is enabled to do by means of a simple "gaff" illustrated in the explanatory diagram. The "steps" upon which the wooden stands rest are covered with velveteen, or some other heavy cloth. Just at the rear of each stand is a small bit of wood, which forms a hump beneath the cloth. The hump, of course, is hidden behind the stand.

To convince the players that they have a fair chance, the operator first drops a ring over one of the wooden stands, to prove that the stand is small enough to accommodate the ring. In removing the ring from the stand, he lifts the stand a trifle, and pushes it back on to the hidden hump. Thus the stand is tilted forward. (The diagram gives an exaggerated view of the forward tilt; in actual practice the lean is hardly noticeable.) The operator then steps out in front of the counter and tosses hoops at the stand. As he is a skilled thrower, he can often land thirty or forty per cent of his throws. In removing the hoops from the stand, the operator draws it back into its normal position. When the player "tries his luck," he is no better off than he was before the operator "demonstrated" the method.

HOOP FALLS ON WHEN STAND IS TILTED FORWARD

The Watch La stands look easy to the player. But they are built to make him lose.

Anyone can hit the ten-pin, but making the coins fly is another story.

The Coin and the Tenpin

A Game That Depends Upon a Scientific Principle Coupled With a Simple "Gaff" That Beats the Players

ONE of the really unique games of the county fair is the "coin and tenpin." It is remarkable for the simplicity of the articles used and the game frequently brings much profit to its owner, because fraud or deception in its operation seems impossible.

A large table or platform is set back behind a counter. In the center of the platform is a black mark, on which the operator carefully sets a tenpin. The tenpin is surrounded by three concentric circles. The innermost has a diameter of about three feet; the next is larger; while the outermost circle touches the edges of the platform, and may be as wide as eight feet in diameter.

The operator sets a silver half dollar flat on top of the tenpin and then walks to the counter. To demonstrate how the game is played, he takes a baseball and throws it at the tenpin. His aim is true. Over goes the pin and the coin flies from the platform.

"There y'are, boys," says the operator. "All ya gotta do is hit the tenpin. Knock the coin outside the first circle, ya get three shots free; knock it outa the second circle, win a quarter; knock it offa the platform like I just done, and I give ya a dollar, three throws for a dime! No fair hittin' the coin when ya throw. Ya gotta hit the pin to make it count. Ya saw me do it; let me see ya do it!"

The hopeful players soon find, however, that it is easy enough to hit the tenpin in one of their three shots, but to knock the coin out of the circle is a different proposition. Occasionally one of the throwers sends the coin outside the inner circle, and receives three more throws as a reward. But the second circle remains uncrossed. Nearly every time the tenpin is hit the coin falls ignominiously inside the innermost circle, even though the pin may fly clear from the platform.

The reason is simple, and you can easily demonstrate the principle on which it is based on your own satisfaction. Set a coin flat on top of an ink bottle. Then pull the bottle away quickly. The coin will not follow the bottle; it will drop straight downward. Precisely the same thing occurs when the tenpin is hit by the baseball. The harder it is struck, the less chance is that the coin will go over the inner circle. If the tenpin is hit lightly, so that it just barely falls, the coin may be thrown over the first circle; but there is little chance that it will travel further, as there is not enough force to propel it.

The wily "bunco man" uses an extra coin, which has a small point soldered to its underside. This point fits in a tiny hole in the top of the tenpin. The "gaffed" coin is set on the tenpin when he is ready to throw. (See explanatory diagrams.) As the projecting point holds the coin to the pin, when the ball strikes the latter, the coin falls along with the pin, and, flying clear of it, rolls outside the furthermost circle. When the players throw the ordinary coin is used; or the "gaffed" coin may be set on the tenpin, but with its projecting point upwards.

The Game Called "Big Tom"

A LARGE cloth figure of a cat is set on a frame-work stand, as shown in the central illustration. All that the player has to do is to hit the tomcat with a baseball and knock it off the stand. Then the patron is given the choice of any article on exhibition; a clock, a doll, a vase, etc. Of course, 10 cents is paid for the privilege of throwing a ball at the cat, or three balls may be thrown for a quarter.

What game could be apparently more fair than this one—especially when a young man steps up and knocks the cat off the rack on his second throw? Simply hit the cat squarely, and it will fall over. Hit it hard and it will fall from the stand.

The explanatory diagrams show how unfair the game really is, and how little chance any one has of

A well-directed throw will knock down the cat, but it always stays on the stand.

knocking the cat from the stand. The cat is heavily weighted near the bottom. When it is set on the stand, as indicated by the heavy line (diagram I), it can be knocked from the stand. For the center of gravity—the point of balance—is near the center of the figure, and when the cat is knocked over, as shown in diagram II, it topples and falls from the stand. This is what happens when the young man throws the ball, and wins a prize. The young man may be a friend of the operator, or he may have been allowed to win in order to arouse the interest of prospective customers.

But when the "easy marks" step up to throw, the operator adopts a different course entirely. In this case, he sets the cat as shown in the dotted line of diagram I. The cat is pushed several inches in front of its first position, and its correct place is easily found by pressing it against a large wooden pin, or peg, which is set in the stand. The pin is hidden from view by the ornamental bit of wood work on the front of the stand.

When the cat is in position of the dotted figure (diagram I), it cannot fall from the stand when it it knocked over. Due to its heavy weight, it falls flat when struck, just as through it were on a hinge.

It remains on the stand, as shown in the dotted figure (diagram II), for its center of gravity (A), is in front of the rear edge of the stand, and it cannot fall off. If the cat were not heavily weighted, a hard blow would cause it to bounce from its position. But the large size of the figure and the lightness of the baseball used prevent such an occurrence.

The Hand Striker

A GAME requiring skill and dexterity usually receives a "big play" when exhibited at a carnival or fair. Such a game is the "Hand Striker," which apparently depends upon the cunningness of the player.

The external appearance of the contrivance is shown in the large drawing. The player strikes the springboard at the base of the upright posts, causing the indicator to travel upward. The numbers on the posts are arranged alternately, so that when the arrow on the right of the indicator is pointing at a number, the arrow on the left is between two numbers. Certain of the numbers are designated as "winners," and if the player is able to strike the indicator so

A—BRAKE
B—SPRINGS
C—RELEASE FOR BRAKE
D—STOPS FOR LOSING NUMBERS
E—STOPS FOR WINNING NUMBERS
F—KNOB TO TURN POST

The Hand Striker is a game that appeals to the skilful player for he does not know that it is set against him.

that it stops at a "winner" he receives a dollar bill in return for the ten cents which he paid for the privilege of striking.

Alongside each number is a notch or stop, which apparently catches the indicator after it has reached the highest point of the stroke. Accordingly, the game develops into an exhibition of skill, with the player attempting to drive the indicator up to one of the winning notches.

The secret mechanism which causes the player to lose is clearly explained in the explanatory diagrams. Note the drawing in which part of the right hand post is cut away, exposing the interior. There lies the secret. Inside the post is an iron rod, having notches, or "stops" on both sides (see large explanatory diagram). It is this rod that actually controls the falling indicator. The visible "stops" out in the wood-work are merely shams. The indicator also has an internal mechanism. "A" represents a metal "brake," which

catches in one of the stops and keeps the indicator from falling. "B" is one of two springs, both of which are released by "C"—a visible part of the mechanism. The players believe that "C" releases the indicator from the visible stops cut in the wood, whereas it actually releases the concealed "brake" from the iron post.

The "stops" are designated by the letters D and E. It will be seen that all of the losing "stops" are on one side of the iron rod, or post, whereas the winning "stops" are all on the other side of the post. At the bottom of the "Striker" is a knob "F" which controls the iron post. This knob is easily reached by the operator from behind the counter. When a "sucker" is playing the game, the operator takes care that the losing stops are all turned toward the indicator. No matter how cleverly the player hits the springboard, the indicator is certain to terminate its trip at one of the losing numbers.

sion, and in the cases of many other spindles, luck has nothing whatever to do with it.

The contrivance is a "set spindle"—a term used to designate spindles which may be "set" so that the player will lose. One authority on gambling devices of this sort claims that there are no spindles in operation at fairs, carnivals, etc., over which the operator has not control. In this case the operator certainly does have control, as the explanatory diagrams reveal.

The pins, or posts, forming the circle of numbered sections, are made of twisted wire. To the casual observer these twists are made merely for ornamental purposes; but there lies the fraud. The diagrams give a side view of one of the pins. It will be noticed that the corkscrew effect gives the pin an inward and an outward curve. The celluloid indicator is just long enough to touch one of the inward points of the pin.

In setting up the pins they are arranged alternately, so that each pin controlling an even section has its inward curve where the odd section pins have outward curves. Accordingly, when the spindle is whirled, the celluloid indicator does not touch the pins controlling the odd-numbered sections. The end of the indicator barely passes by them, so it is bound to terminate at an even-numbered section.

The post on which the arrow spins may be slightly raised (as indicated in the diagrams), by lifting on a lever which protrudes from the rear of the board on which the spindle is mounted. With a touch of his finger the operator can secretly raise the arrow a fraction of an inch. This causes the indicator to connect with the inward curves of the odd-numbered sections, and to miss the even numbers entirely. Thus, whether the player plays the odds or the evens, the operator can see to it that no prize will be forthcoming.

Instead of raising the entire wooden arrow by the concealed

The Whirling Spindle

THE spindle described in this article is sometimes termed the "improved spindle," as it represents the latest word in efficiency, attained by the makers of "gaffed" spindles. In appearance, the spindle is a heavy wooden arrow, mounted on a wooden base. Protruding from the end of the arrow is an indicator made of stout celluloid. This is just long enough to touch a circle of posts, or pins, which are set around the axis of the arrow, and which form a circle of numbered sections, alternating odd and even. When the spindle is whirled it spins around rapidly, finally coming to a stop. The celluloid indicator, which has been striking the pins during the rapid revolution, indicates the winning section. The

arrow is always spun in the same direction; usually from left to right, and the player may spin it himself. But, strange though it may seem, he never manages to win any of the valuable prizes which are displayed before his eyes. He is told that if his spin stops on an even number, he will win. But every whirl seems to terminate on an odd section. Then he places his money on the odd numbers, and the arrow invariably comes to rest with the indicator pointing to an even numbered section.

Most unsuccessful players attribute their losses to bad luck. Rarely do they suspect the operator of fraud, for everything seems fair and "on the level." But in the case of the spindle under discus-

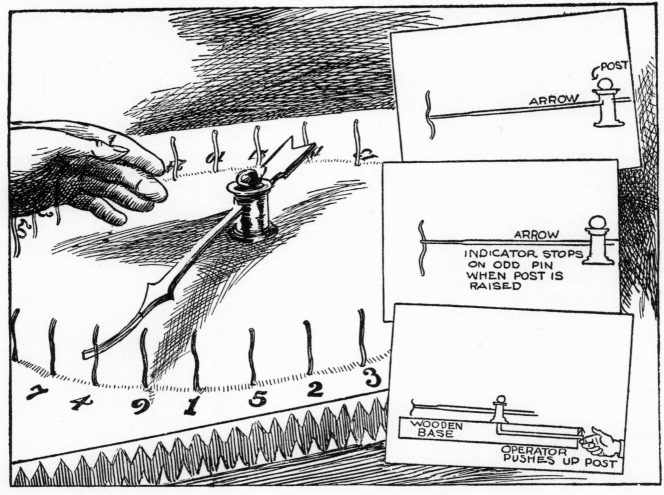

The spindle looks fair, but the operator can control it.

lever, some spindles have an inner post at the axis of the arrow. This post is connected to the celluloid indicator, which is not set in the tip of the arrow, but runs to the axis just underneath the arrow and whirls with the arrow. By raising or lowering the lever the operator controls the indicator, and there is no actual raising of the arrow itself.

It must be remembered that in many cases the operator of a spindle game or a wheel has his game figured out on a percentage basis and does not have to worry as long as he has plenty of players. Some people have the erroneous impression that a percentage game is not a swindle, but, as a matter of fact, it generally is, even when run on the level.

If a man went into a store and received thirty cents' worth of **merchandise** for a payment of a

Phoney Advertisements

AN advertisement which has appeared and caught the suckers reads something like this:

PORTRAIT OF GEORGE WASHINGTON

Made from steel engravings. Finest workmanship. Authentic portrait issued by the United States government. We have a small supply of these which were received in a slightly damaged condition, and will sell them at the price of $1.00 each.

BUNKUM ART STUDIO
3520 Anywhere Street
Philadelphia, Pa.

The person who sends a dollar for one of these portraits receives, by return mail, a lightly cancelled two-cent stamp!

dollar and a half he would certainly feel that he had been swindled by the storekeeper. Yet that is just what happens to players who tackle the wheels and spindles. Fifteen of them put up a dime apiece and the winner gets a prize worth about thirty cents.

Of course, the players see the prize—and they can figure out the percentage of the wheel if they wish to do so, but that does not alter the circumstances. The operator is constantly creating the impression that he is giving a big prize worth a dollar or more. Misrepresentation is but one of his many offenses.

By using a crooked wheel or spindle the operator can offer big special prizes and make one hundred per cent profit. That is why so many of the percentage games have their "gaff" always ready.

"Pop 'Em in the Bucket"

TOSS 'em in the bucket, boys! Win a blanket for a dime!" This is a familiar cry of the carnival fakir as he stands behind his counter and points to a small bucket that protrudes, at an angle, from an open netting.

As a prospective customer stops in front of the stand the operator is quick to demonstrate the simplicity of the game. For the small sum of ten cents the player is provided with three soft baseballs. His object is to toss the balls, one at a time, into the bucket, which is about fifteen feet away from him (see illustration). The balls, however, must not bounce out of the bucket but must stay inside and roll out of the hole at the bottom of the bucket.

Sometimes the operator will engage in a contest with an excep-

tionally clever player. Each man tosses a dozen balls at a different bucket and the one totaling the highest score wins a specified sum. Needless to say, the operator invariably wins by a decisive margin.

The "pop-'em-in" game is a very deceptive one and even without the employment of a "gaff" or secret contrivance the player's chances become practically nil, as considerable skill is required to toss the balls successfully. The player who makes two successful tosses is apt to lose his nerve on the third throw and as each toss must be made almost perfectly, he is doomed to failure.

But the grafting operator is not satisfied to rely on the player's inability. He prefers to "play the game safe." Hence, the "pop-'em-in" game is often controlled by a "gaff" that takes away even the

slight chance that the player has of winning.

The explanatory diagram illustrates a typical method by which this is accomplished. The bucket has a double bottom, the lower of which may be slightly lowered, if desired. When the two bottoms are pressed together the bottom of the bucket is so firm that any ball striking it, even at the slightest angle, will be certain to bounce out of the bucket. The lower bottom is connected, as illustrated, with a lever which runs across the front of the bucket-rack, and which appears to be an ordinary foot rest. By stepping on one end of the lever the operator causes the lower bottom to sink. When the bucket is so arranged it is not unduly difficult to "pop-'em-in." Thus the operator can demonstrate the game and show "how easy it is."

"Pop 'em in," shouts the operator, but the players "pop 'em out."

The Well Known String Game

THE operator of the "String Game" is usually a young woman, who very obligingly consents to explain the game. Any one who pays a dime is privileged to pick out any string among the tangled ends which the operator holds in her hand. (See illustration.) The string is drawn loose from the others, and when the player pulls on it, his prize is raised from the rack, is detached from the string, and is given to him.

To demonstrate the fairness of the game, the operator pulls on the entire bunch of strings. All of the prizes, large and small, are raised from the rack by this action, thus proving that every string is a "live one." If any one points out a large prize that suits his fancy, the operator, by following the course of the string from the crossbar to her hand, can pick out the string and show that it is attached to the desired prize, and that the loose end is actually among those in her hand.

But should a casual observer station himself a short distance away and watch the game in progress during an evening, he would be surprised at the small number of large prizes won during an evening's play. As a matter of fact, the rack would probably be just as well stocked with "big winners" at the end of the evening as it was before the game opened for business.

The deception employed in the "String Game" is amusingly simple, but remarkably efficient. It is clearly exposed in the explanatory diagram. The operator, before opening the game, doubles back the loose ends of the strings which are attached to the larger prizes. These loose ends form a tangled mass and the doubled ends are concealed therein.

When a player approaches the counter the operator grasps the tangled strings about two inches from the ends. Thus the double-back strings are safely held in her hand and the unsuspecting player has absolutely no chance of winning a "big one." As all of the strings actually run into the operator's hand, she can lift the entire collection of prizes by merely pulling the bunched strings. She can also trace the course of any string from the prize, over the crossbar and down to her hand.

There is no "gaff" or secret contrivance; nothing can get out of order; a child can operate the game. Hence the wives and daughters of many concession operators are often employed in the swindling of the general public and join the great host of charlatans and rogues who annually collect thousands of dollars from the patrons of fairs and carnivals.

STRINGS TURNED BACK ARE THE LARGE PRIZES

STRINGS THAT HANG DOWN ARE SMALL PRIZES

Every string is attached to a prize; this is demonstrated to the players.

The thrill of a Kentucky derby is packed into this miniature race course.

The Miniature Race Course

A Percentage Game That Can Be Controlled—"Playing the Ponies" at the Carnival or Fair

"THEY'RE off!"

The crowd leans forward and all eyes are on the horses as they start around the track. Faster and faster they go. Then the operator drops the crank and lets the horses continue their mad dash around the circle unaided. For the horses are pigmy ponies made of metal and the track is a mechanical "race course," the latest device of the ever-ingenious bunco man.

Each horse is numbered and each player places a dime or a quarter on a selected horse. When the horses are "covered" the operator turns a crank, which revolves a metal table underneath the top of the box. The horses whirl around at a great rate. When they have attained their maximum

speed the operator releases the crank and lets the momentum carry on the race.

This is where the interest begins. The horses slow down their pace and finally come to a complete stop. Then the winner is determined by means of a crossbar marked "Finish." The horse whose neck is nearest to the bar is pronounced the winner. If a horse has just passed under the bar, he is disqualified. The winning horse must always be approaching the bar.

The game may be, and often is, played on a percentage basis with no element of fraud involved except the foisting of cheap prizes off on the winners who think, at first sight, that they are receiving something really worth while.

But, unfortunately, everything is not always "on the level," and the bunco man is able to more than double his profits by "gaffing" the game. How he does it is plainly revealed by a study of the inner mechanism of the race course, that part of the game which is always out of sight of the unwitting public.

When the operator turns the crank that starts the race he is turning a fly-wheel made of metal, which acts on a gear (see explanatory diagram). The gear revolves the heavy metal table which is under the top of the box and in which the horses are attached.

A metal rod runs up through the stand upon which the race course is set, terminating at the rim of the fly-wheel. At the bottom of the rod is a foot lever. Setting his foot on this lever the operator keeps a sharp eye on the horses as they slow down their course. One or more of these

horses has been covered by a "shill"—a confederate of the operator—who is in the crowd. Just as the "shill's" horse approaches the finish line the operator presses

on the pedal and applies the brake. The confederate's horse is the winner. He receives the prize and returns it to the operator at the close of the evening.

The Game of Red, White and Blue

Introducing the Tricky Dealer's Ball That Appears Often and Wins Plenty

THE unscrupulous gamesters who frequent fairs and carnivals are ever ready to employ any means at their disposal that will bring "suckers" to their booths. In the "Red, White and Blue" game they frequently appeal to patriotic sentiment to obtain players. A booth bedecked with bags and tri-color trimmings is certain to attract attention, and wherever this game is

operated its proprietors lead most of the other games in making money.

The game consists of a wooden box with a sliding top. Five red balls, five white and five blue, each less than an inch in diameter, are dropped into the box. (See Figure A.) They are followed by a white ball with a red stripe—called the "dealer's ball."

On the "laydown," an oilcloth

strip along the counter, are three squares—one red, one white and one blue. The patrons of the game place their money on the different squares. Then the box is tilted slightly forward and a sliding door in the front of the box is pushed up. This door is just large enough to allow one ball to roll out. (See illustration.) If the ball is red, all the players who have money on that color are paid "double

The color of the ball that rolls out indicates the winner.

money." That is, for every dollar they have placed on the red square they receive two dollars additional. The white and blue players lose their money.

The ball that has rolled out is replaced in the box and the box is shaken and again tilted forward, while money is placed on the three squares. Occasionally the dealer's ball rolls out. Then all of the players lose their money and every dollar put on the "laydown" goes to the dealer. This is supposed to be his profit for operating the game—one dollar out of sixteen. In other words, the game is a simplified form of roulette, where there are two "blanks" on the wheel of thirty-six numbers.

It is obvious that, if the dealer's ball can be made to appear about one in five times, or when unusu- ally large stakes are on the counter the operator's profits will undergo an enormous increase. Diagrams "B" and "C" show how the operator brings this to pass. The dealer's ball is coated with steel while the other balls are made of a composition resembling ivory. Inside the sliding door of the box is a strong magnet. When the balls are all in the box the dealer lets them all roll to the front, where they pile up and press against the sliding door. Then he tilts the box backward slightly. All the balls roll to the rear of the box with the exception of the dealer's ball, which remains affixed to the door. Naturally, when the balls are again rolled to the front and the door is slid up the striped ball will roll forth and the operator will clean up the counter.

Throwing Darts

An Emergency Game of "Science and Skill" Seen on Every Midway

THE general appearance of the dart game is shown in the illustration. A square board stands upright behind a counter. The player is given an unlimited supply of darts and is told to toss until he wins. On the board are a number of tags, arranged in regular rows. When the player has succeeded in impaling one of the tags it is removed from the hook, and its reverse side is exhibited. On the reverse side is a number between one and one hundred, or between one and sixty-four. If the player has struck one of the lucky numbers he receives a "big prize"—one of the articles shown in the drawing. But if any other number appears on the tag he is rewarded with a tin whistle, a pair of celluloid spectacles, a collar button or some other article of insignificant value.

On the board, illustrated there are sixty-four tags, and nine or ten "big winners." This, apparently, gives the player about one chance in eight of landing a large prize. As the latter are worth more than a dollar apiece the percentage, apparently, is in favor of the player. Such would, indeed, be the case if there were any winning numbers on the tags. But, unfortunately for the player, there is not a single winning tag. Nine of the tags are duplicates of losing tags, so that the operator never finds it necessary to replenish his stock of big prizes.

Such a bold-faced swindle could never be perpetrated but for an ingenious ruse that the operator adopts to make the players think that the nine winning tags are actually on the board. A reference to the explanatory diagram will give an insight into the artifice employed by the unscrupulous operator.

It will be noticed that all of the "winning numbers" end in one or zero. The numbers on the tags are rather crudely made and are all out of proportion. Thus, when the operator removes a tag numbered twenty-seven and exhibits it to the players, he has merely to place the tip of his thumb on the bar of the seven and the number appears to be twenty-one. In the same manner numbers eighteen, fifty-seven, nineteen and thirty-nine may be shown as numbers ten, fifty-one, eleven and thirty-one respectively.

The operator has a "shill," or confederate, who mingles with the crowd. This man tosses a dart and impales number eighteen. The operator removes the tag, shows it as number ten, and reluctantly gives one of the "big prizes" to the "shill," who walks away in triumph. The operator shows a few other tags, exhibiting them as "winners," and the spectators are soon induced to try the game. Often a player will notice where a winning tag was placed. He will toss his darts at that tag. Probably he will strike a few other tags and be forced to take small prizes before he attains his desired tag. But when the tag is shown to him it is not a "winner" at all. He naturally comes to the conclusion that he was mistaken and walks away in disgust.

When the operator sees a player who he thinks is a "sucker" he often resorts to special measures which will bring him a big profit. He waits until the player has spent a dollar on the game, then he draws the player aside and tells him that he may toss at a rate of twenty-five cents instead of a mere dime and that if he is successful he will not only receive a large prize, but will have all of his losses returned. The player willingly accepts this plan, and soon has spent about two dollars more in using up the number of chances which the op-

"Throw until you win," shouts the operator; but no one wins a big prize.

erator has granted him "as a special favor" because he is a "regular fellow."

The operator tells him to toss without charge. The spectator soon impales one of the tricky tags. The operator removes it and lays it, number side down, on the counter. He tells the player that for fifty cents he may have the tag, and if it is a "winner" all of his losses will be returned. If the player will not take a chance, the "shill" steps up and offers to buy the tag for fifty cents. This unexpected competition will often force the "sucker" to buy. But if he still refuses, the tag is sold to the confederate and the operator exhibits it as a "winner." The confederate is paid and the "sucker," seeing his success, agrees to continue playing on a fifty-cent basis. Sometimes he is even drawn up to a "dollar game," and many a man has tossed away his week's pay in this manner.

The Wheel of Chance

Giving the Odds Against a Player in a Percentage Game and Explaining the "Gaff"

ONE of the most common sights of the country fair grounds is the "Wheel of Chance," or "P. C. (percentage) Wheel," as it is known among the gamesters. Wherever games of chance are permitted the "P. C. Wheels" will appear in abundance, for, despite the increasing popularity of the more modern games, the old-fashioned wheel still holds its own.

The playing of the game is simplicity itself. The players "cover" the numbers on the "laydown" with dimes or larger coins. Then the operator whirls the wheel. The

leather indicator at the top of the wheel bounces up and down as each nail goes by; finally, the wheel comes to a stop, and the section in which the leather indicator rests is the "winning section."

The player who has "covered" the winning number is paid according to which sub-division the indicator points; if the dollar section is indicated, he receives one dollar for every dime he placed on the counter; if 50 or 30 are indicated, he receives fifty or thirty cents, respectively.

It should now be clear why the game is called a "Percentage

SIDE VIEW

THUMB TACK
WITH LEAD
SOLDERED ON HEAD

The Wheel of Chance pays a definite percentage to the operator.

Wheel." The operator is sure, in the long run, of steady profits, gained through a favorable percentage. Suppose all eight sections are covered with a dime. The operator takes in eighty cents. In five spins of the wheel his receipts will total $4. According to the law of averages, he will pay out $1 once, fifty cents twice, thirty cents twice, a total of $2.60, which nets him a profit of $1.40.

There are certain times when the operator can manipulate the wheel to good advantage. Suppose he is experiencing a "bloomer," which is carnival parlance for a bad week. No one who visits his booth seems to have money. He is paying a large rental for the privilege of operating his wheel, and he must meet expenses. Finally, one man comes along who exhibits plenty of money and is ready to play the game on a large scale. He places a $5 bill on one of the numbers,

figuring that he can win from $15 to $50. The operator sees a chance to win $5 clear, and he prefers

to rely on his own ingenuity rather than on the uncertain laws of chance. He spins the wheel: the victim loses, and the operator pockets the $5.

The explanatory diagram, which gives a side view of the wheel, exposes the simple expedient used by the operator. An ordinary thumb tack, with a piece of lead soldered to the head, does the trick. He deftly inserts the tack on the rear of the wheel at a point directly in back of the number played by the "sucker." Naturally, the wheel comes to rest with the player's number at the bottom.

A story is told of how a carnival operator was "double crossed" by a man who painted his wheel. The painter inserted a weight in the wheel so that it would always turn up a certain number. Then he sent a man to the carnival to play that number with the result that he brought back all the prizes.

The color board offers attractive prizes that never pass across the counter.

The Game of Color Combination
How the Law of Averages Works Against the Player

THE board shown in the illustration comprises five colors: red, white, green, blue and black. The board is divided into fifty sections, like an egg crate. In each section is a wooden cube with a metal knob on top, which enables the operator to lift it from its section. The bottom of each cube is painted in one of the five colors; thus there are ten cubes of each color.

The operator arranges his cubes in a haphazard way and then waits for customers. The player pays a nickel and is given his choice of five cubes. They are removed from their sections and are laid on the counter. The color combinations are noted and the player receives a prize according to the chart which hangs in the background.

The player will often spend from 50 cents to $2 on this game and he usually departs without a box of candy.

The reason is simple. The law of averages is overwhelmingly in favor of the operator. The player's chances of winning a box of candy are approximately as follows:

Five different colors (five-pound box of candy)—less than one chance in 2,000.

Five of any one color (three-pound box)—less than one in 1,500.

Four of any one color (one-pound box)—about one in fifty.

Three of one color, two of another (half-pound box)—about one in twenty.

Thus the operator takes in $1 for every half-pound box he delivers. The box costs him about fifteen cents. For every pound box, valued at thirty cents, he takes in $2.50. Thus in receiving $5 he delivers five half-pounds and two one pounds, a total outlay of $1.20. The three and five-pound boxes are not considered. The operator takes in more than $75 for every three-pound box, and more than $100 for every five-pound box.

Some operators keep lookout for individual "suckers," whom they can swindle on a larger scale. When a likely prospect approaches the operator lets him see where five of the red cubes are placed. Accordingly the player is ready to bet heavily that he can pick out five cubes of one color. But in two of the sections where the cubes were set there lay a flat square of tin (see explanatory diagram) with four sharp points projecting upwards. The bottom of one tin square is painted green, the other blue. By merely pressing on the cubes the square becomes firmly attached to the bottom of each cube, thus transforming them from red to green and blue, respectively, and arranging a surprise for the "sucker" when the cubes are removed.

The Six Ball Roll Down Board
It Lures Unsuspecting Players and Takes Their Cash

A BOARD six feet in length is set at a slight slant, as shown in the large illustration. At the outer end of the board is a ledge or rack which contains six cork balls, each two and a half inches in diameter. The player, upon payment of a dime, is allowed to tip up the ledge, whereupon the balls roll down the incline. Each ball settles in one of thirty-six pockets, which are numbered from one to six, inclusive—there being six holes of each number.

When the balls have all settled in holes the operator adds up the totals. On a large chart are listed the winning totals. Numbers 6, 7 and 8; 34, 35 and 36 win big prizes. Numbers 9, 10 and 11; 31, 32 and 33 win medium prizes. But, strange to relate, the players do not win the prizes. Numbers 12, 13 and 14; 28, 29 and 30 win small prizes, and several of the players win one or more of these. But as each small prize has a retail value of ten or fifteen cents the operator can afford to lose them.

A study of the lower explanatory diagram will show how greatly the percentages favor the operator. In order to score from 6 to 11 the player must put one or more balls into the number 1 holes. To score from 31 to 36 he must pocket one or more balls in the number 6 holes.

All of the 1 and 6 pockets are at the sides of the board, with the intermediate numbers at the middle. When the balls roll down they do not spread to the sides but form a somewhat uneven line straight across the board. On the average

When the ledge is tipped the balls roll into the numbered holes.

the player will pocket 1, 2, 3, 4, 5 and 6, a total of 21. Perhaps he may make two sixes and two fives, instead of the one and the two. This will give him a score of 6, 5, 3, 4, 5, 6—totaling 29. That is about the best score that he can hope for. It will win him a small prize, but will fall two points short of the coveted 31, which carries with it a medium prize.

Suppose the player rolls five balls into the number 6 holes. The bunco man quickly notes this fact and steps up to count the player's score. He lifts one of the balls from one of the number 6 holes, as shown in the upper explanatory diagram. As he draws the ball back a few inches and calls out "six," his hand comes directly over the next ball, which is also

in a number 6 hole. His hand and the ball he holds obscure the player's view. With a slight flip of his finger he cleverly rolls the rear ball out of its hole and into the number 1 hole behind it. Thus, when he comes to count up that ball it is scored as "one," and the player's total is diminished beyond repair.

The Standard Spindle Game

How an Automatic Device Controls the Supposed Percentage and Makes Spindle Spell Swindle

THE most modern "bunco games" frequently incorporate "gaffs," or secret contrivances, that are masterpieces of simplicity and ingenuity. Certain manufacturers turn out these games in large quantities every season and charge high prices for their goods; but the bunco men do not quibble about overcharges, for they know that a really up-to-date game will bring them enormous

The spindle pays the operator a percentage, but he can control it also.

profits and one day's earnings will often pay the initial cost of the game.

Suppose a half a dozen "sports" saunter up to the "spindle game." The operator leans across the counter and confidentially tells them that he is no "cheap skate." He asserts that he is a "regular fellow" and will run his game on a man-size scale. Each of the "sports" is induced to lay a dollar on a compartment; the prize at stake is a $20 bill. Or if they prefer to risk $2 each a $50 bill will be forthcoming to the winner. The operator produces the "fifty" and slips it under the edge of the board.

The players are quick to realize that the odds are greatly in their favor. Each man has only one chance in ten of winning, but if he wins, he obtains twenty-five times as much as he put up. The numbers are quickly covered with one or two vacancies, which belong to the operator and represent his sole chances of winning. But when the arrow is whirled it comes to rest on a "blank" and the operator takes in the cash.

The explanatory diagram shows the "gaff" in detail. The arrow, which is perfectly balanced, sets in a socket, from which it may be lifted at any time. The board is a plain piece of wood, painted and covered with oilcloth, which is held taut by thumb tacks around the sides. But from the rear of the board, straight through to the center there is a long hole. This hole contains a rod (shown in the diagram), to the end of which is soldered the head of a thumb tack. Everything may be inspected, but the "gaff" will never be detected. While the arrow is spinning, the operator rests his hand on the edge of the board. His thumb presses against the thumb tack at the end of the rod and as the arrow slows down he presses the rod just as the arrow points to a section covered by himself or his confederate. The rod pushes the pivot (or axle of the arrow) against the side of the socket, and the arrow stops on the operator's number.

The Game of English Pool

THIS is a game that wins plenty from unsophisticated people. There are many poolroom sharks who will take a chance on it, because it looks easy.

The game is played on a board about four feet long and a foot and a half wide. At one end is a chalk line; at the other a painted circle, with a pocket beyond.

Two pool balls are used. One is set in the middle of the circle, and three coins are placed upon it in a stack. The player is provided with a cue, and the object is for him to shoot another ball and knock the ball out of the circle.

If all the coins drop within the circle, the player gets nothing for his trouble; but if one, two or three coins fly outside the ring, he is paid a small, medium or large prize, accordingly.

Of course, he pays ten cents for the privilege of shooting; and that seems small enough. The game looks easy, but it doesn't work in practice. The coins always drop within the circle. It is inter-

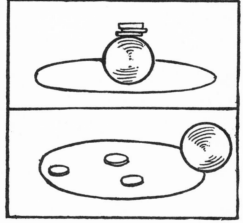

How the coins are stacked on the ball, and how they fall in the circle.

esting to watch a pool player at this game. He studies his shots; tries hard shots, easy ones, draws, English and cushion shots; but he can't seem to get the combination that will do the trick.

Sometimes a very easy shot may help, but as a rule the player prefers a straight drive. The harder he drives the less chance does he have of winning. The ball flies out from beneath the balanced coins and their tendency is to drop straight down to the board.

The billiard expert will keep at this game, and it is very profitable to the owner, for he simply sits by and takes in the dimes. A player who knows how to handle the cue hates to admit defeat.

But straight pool and English pool are entirely different games. Knocking the coins out of the ring is almost a hopeless task; because when the ball is struck it shoots

The board used in the English pool game.

so quickly that the coins are bound to drop straight down.

Sometimes the operator demonstrates the game and shows how easy it is. He used a coin that has a little wax on the under side. It is the bottom coin of the stack. When he hits the ball the coin goes with it for a short distance, and as a result two or three of the coins fall outside of the mystic circle.

The large illustration shows the appearance of the game; the explanatory diagram shows the balancing of the coins.

The Tricky Tumbler bounces down the board.   The "gaff" is shown at the right.

The Tricky Tumbler

THE Tricky Tumbler is a small carnival game which may also be used in arcades and museums. It is apparently a real example of a game requiring "science and skill."

The whole apparatus consists of an inclined board with a bumper at the lower end and a hole near the same end. Besides this, a capsule-shaped tumbler is used. It has a shifting weight, so that when it is given a slight push and is started down the slanting board it will turn a series of somersaults.

Tumblers of this sort are not new; they have been used in many innocent games sold in the stores, as there is great amusement in trying to make the eccentric tumbler bound into a destination. In fact, the tumbling game illustrated in the large picture is very similar to a game played by children.

The man who operates this game has learned to demonstrate it to perfection, and he can make the tumbler bounce into the hole time after time. There is something fascinating about the game, and it looks so easy that players are willing to take a chance, especially as a prize is offered as a reward. Of course it costs a nickel or a dime to enter the game.

Time and again the player will roll the little tumbler and will watch it turn end over end on its way to the destination. But never will it come to rest in the hole, even though the player may spend four or five dollars on the game.

The reason why is shown in the explanatory drawing. A secret device in the side of the board enables the operator to enlarge or decrease the size of the hole. The change is not great; it is, however, sufficient to keep the tumbler from bouncing in when the player starts it rolling. But when the operator takes a chance he has the switch the right way, and the tumbler can be bounced into the hole.

The mechanical construction of this contrivance is made very neatly, so that it will not create suspicion. It is virtually impossible to detect the operator when he is working it. Sometimes two tumblers can be used — one a trifle larger and more eccentric than the other. This enables the operator to work with an ordinary board, switching one tumbler for the other —letting the players use the bad one, while he works with the good one.

A board of this sort measures more than four feet in length and is nearly a foot in width. So it makes an attractive display and gets the players. At the same time it sets up easily and quickly, which is why many bunco men use it. When you see this game in operation watch it if you wish and keep your eye on the operator. But no matter how unconcerned he may appear, don't risk your cash. You will be sure to lose it, so what's the use?

The Game of Fish Pond

The Little Fish Are in the Pool—But the Big Fish Is the Player—"Nobody Loses"—But the Operator Wins

THE game of "Fish Pond" is one of the prettiest and most interesting of all carnival concessions. It is an elaborate affair that requires a considerable outlay of money on the part of the operator, and hence it is usually seen on the "midway" of the larger fairs.

The large drawing shows the game in operation. A stream of water, flowing down a narrow channel, carries along with it a hundred wooden fish. Attached to each fish is a bit of wire, terminating in a large loop. The player is provided with a fishing rod, a hook and line. He pays ten cents for the privilege of "hooking a fish."

When the player has drawn forth a fish the operator takes it from the end of the player's line and, swinging back an overlapping piece of wood on the bottom of the fish, reveals a number (see explanatory diagram). If the number

"Hook your fish and win a prize"—but you will never get a big one!

RING BY WHICH CUSTOMER CATCHES FISH ON HOOK—

BOTTOM OF FISH SHOWING NUMBER

corresponds with any of the ten winning numbers (see large drawing), the player wins a "big prize." The fish are numbered from 1 to 100.

But, strange to say, the player never succeeds in landing a big number. The operator, however, can always catch a fish of value when he takes the pole to show "how easy it is."

The explanatory diagram reveals the secret and shows how the player (as one operator has termed it) makes a "sucker of himself. The numbers are not neatly stamped on the bottom of the fish, but are crudely scratched or engraved. If the overlap is not completely swung aside any ordinary number can be shown as a "winner." Thus the operator can always win, but when his victim catches a fish the overlap is completely swung aside and an ordinary number is revealed.

The ten winning fish do not appear "in the swim." They are retained inside the opening at the left of the counter where the fish emerge, but can be released when desired in case the game should be investigated by the authorities. After the fish traverse the length of the counter the channel continues back underneath the counter and the fish are lifted up by machinery to start their journey once again. Thus a perpetual stream of fish is continually floating by to fill the demands of the perpetual stream of "suckers" who place their good money on the game, and the operator, not the customer, "hooks the poor fish."

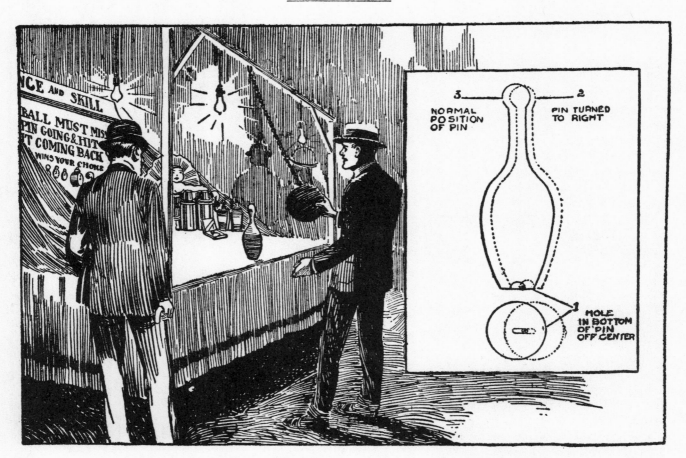

Swing the ball forward and hit the pin coming back. That is the rule of the game.

The Swinging Ball and the Ten-Pin

HANGING from a wooden framework is a regulation bowling ball, suspended by a light chain. A tenpin is standing on the counter beside the spot where the ball normally hangs.

The operator takes the ball and gives it a deft swing past the tenpin, the ball just missing the pin. On its return swing the ball strikes the pin cleanly and knocks it off the counter.

The ball swings freely on the frame; there is no "fake" there. Everything seems fair enough and the player is soon induced to "take a chance" at ten cents a swing. He takes careful aim and swings the ball with a deftness imitative of the operator. But the ball, on its return swing, misses the tenpin by the fraction of an inch. Again the player attempts it; again the slightest margin of space prevents him from attaining success. Finally he gives up, after he has expended time, energy and money. Then he sees the operator swing the ball again and send the pin flying from the counter.

"The Swinging Ball" is one of the most popular of all the devices which bunco the public, and very often two or three of them are seen in operation at one carnival. The reason why a "joint" of this type appeals to the unscrupulous operator is because the disgruntled player seldom protests.

A study of the explanatory diagrams will reveal the secret of the contrivance. The secret does not lie in the ball, but in the pin itself, the hole in the bottom of the tenpin (which serves as the guide to set it upon the nail in the center) is bored slightly off center. Thus the tenpin may be set two ways: either as indicated in the solid line or as shown in the dotted line. The normal position of the pin is that indicated by the solid line, with the bulk of the pin to the left of the nail in the counter. (See point 1.)

The operator starts the ball swinging from point 2, just to the right of the pin. On its return trip the ball comes along at point 3, and if the swing is well executed, the pin will be struck by the side of the ball.

But suppose the tenpin is turned as shown in the dotted figure! The ball, started at point 2, must begin its swing about one-half an inch further to the right than it does when the pin is in its normal position. This means that it will describe a greater arc in its swing. In other words it will come about one inch farther to the left when it reaches point 3. Thus it becomes almost a physical impossibility to hit the pin when it is "off center."

The hawker's valise does the trick.

Selling Soap

A Pet Swindle of the Street Faker

STREET fakers use many artful dodges in dispensing their goods. Sometimes they sell legitimate merchandise, but they frequently dispose of cheap articles at "bargain" prices, and in so doing make more profit than a legitimate merchant. In cities where regulations are in force very few bunco games are worked on the streets, but in other places the street hawkers put over some questionable deals.

When it comes to buying a ten-cent balloon from a man on the street there is no hoax; but when a glib talker is demonstrating a new kind of stain remover or massage cream there is a large chance that the wonderful article he is selling for fifty cents cost him a thin dime or less.

These smooth salesmen often employ surprising methods to start the sale going. They may give away an article to the first man who puts up his money; or they may use the special premium plan that has been used chiefly by the soap sellers.

The vender opens a suitcase and places it on a folding table. He harangues the passers-by and soon draws a crowd. The article he is selling is soap—a very fine brand, so he says—at a price ranging from twenty-five to fifty cents a cake.

The onlookers are interested; but none of them care to spend their money, despite the fact that the seller calls the soap a bargain. So the faker asks the people to gather up close while he makes the offer profitable in solid cash. He states that he will give away money to lucky buyers, and the people become interested.

Taking out a cake of soap, the faker opens the wrapper and puts money in it. Sometimes he inserts a coin—a half dollar or even a gold piece. On other occasions, he unwraps a bar of soap and folds a dollar bill or a five spot in the wrapper, which he replaces on the cake.

This makes the spectators open their eyes, and after the hawker has treated ten or a dozen cakes of soap in this generous manner everyone is ready for business.

The faker puts the cakes of soap back in the bag, and shakes all the contents. Then he states that he will sell the bars of soap at twenty-five cents apiece to all customers. Right away people put up their money. Some take two, three, or four cakes of soap.

One man quickly opens his bar of soap and finds a dollar bill. The faker stops the sale for a moment and tells the purchasers not to look inside until after he has sold more cakes; otherwise the sale will

be destroyed, and the premium value will be lost.

Nevertheless, most of the customers open their cakes of soap on the sly. The cakes with the money wrapped inside are not found. The customers know they must be in the bag, and they come back for more. The faker sells a hundred cakes of five-cent soap in ten minutes.

Then the bag is empty. He closes it, picks up his table and moves on, leaving the lucky purchasers to find their money. The ground is strewn with opened soap-wrappers, but not a cent of money is discovered, and when the last bar of soap has been uncovered the crowd realizes that they have been stung.

Some of these fakers are clever enough to extract the money by

palming it as they wrap each cake of soap. The man who finds money in the wrapper is a confederate, although sometimes the faker lets two or three bars get by in order to do more business.

Another method of getting rid of the money is shown in the explanatory diagram. The faker has a large suitcase, and there is a pocket or compartment in the side. That is toward the crowd, and they do not see the bunco man drop each cake of money-laden soap into the pocket. The soap he sells is wrapped in plain packages, and he can show the bag empty when he concludes the sale. Then he departs with his table and his bag, carrying all the wrapped-up bills away in the secret compartment of the satchel.

The Lucky Pocketbook

The Game That Makes the Suckers Bite — The Mysterious Coin That Goes and Comes

IT is impossible to tell where the game of "lucky pocketbook" first originated. It has been worked time and again in poolrooms, barber shops, saloons, cigar stores and other places where men are wont to assemble.

It starts among a group of men who are talking together. One of them makes his departure and on the chair where he has been seated someone spies an odd-shaped pocketbook.

"Jack must have dropped that," he says.

"Yes, that belongs to him," says another man. "He calls it his lucky pocketbook. He carries an old dime in it that has the date of the year he was born."

Someone opens the pocketbook. Sure enough, there is the dime.

"He'll be back for it, I guess," says someone.

"Of course he will," replies another.

"Let's work a joke on him," says the man who mentioned the lucky dime. "We'll take out the lucky dime and see if he misses it."

That is done and the pocketbook is placed in a counter to await the return of the owner.

Soon Jack arrives on the scene, breathless, with a worried look on his face. He sees the pocketbook and picks it up.

"That your pocketbook?" asks someone. "Must have a lot of money in it, the way you were anxious to get it."

"Nothing in it but a dime," answers Jack, as he starts to put the pocketbook in his pocket. "But I wouldn't lose that dime. It's a lucky one. It has the date 1899. Always brings me good luck."

Some person laughs.

"You don't mean to say that you came back in such a hurry just for a thin dime!"

can't imagine what has happened.

The game has been carefully prepared beforehand. Jack has a confederate in the crowd, who acts as the "come on" man. He suggests the removal of the dime and starts the joke on Jack. In his pocket Jack has another pocketbook, containing a dime of the proper date. He starts to put the empty pocketbook away, drops it in his pocket and brings out the duplicate that contains the coin.

Sometimes a trick pocketbook is used with a pocket in the side, holding the duplicate dime. Then it is not necessary for the owner even to touch the pocketbook after he comes back.

The two swindlers meet later and divide their spoils. If they know how to put it across, this game brings them tidy profits whenever it is worked.

There are many variations to this game and it would be impossible to explain all the various swindles that have been practiced by clever sharpers. But many of the ones that are apparently new are merely modern developments of the old ones—for, after all, there is very little new under the sun. The safe plan is to watch out for any little bet that looks like a sure thing.

Working the Lucky Pocketbook. The diagram shows the "switch."

"That's what I said," responds Jack hotly. "A dime with the date 1899!"

"You've got to show me," says one of the crowd. "I'll bet you haven't got a dime marked 1899 in that pocketbook."

Jack starts to open the pocketbook. Then he throws it down on the table with a sharp oath.

"What do you want to bet?" he demands angrily.

The gang gets interested. Here is where they have some fun with Jack.

"I'll bet you a dollar that there's no such dime in the pocketbook," says one.

"Piker," shouts Jack, pulling a wad of bills from his pocket. "I'll bet any man in the place ten dollars on it. Why, I've carried that dime in my pocketbook all my life!"

The bets are on. Everyone in the crowd sees some easy money. Each one covers a ten-spot of Jack's money. Then he calls on some person to open the pocketbook. Everyone smiles. The pocketbook is opened and out drops a dime. It bears the date 1899. Jack picks it up, puts it in his pocketbook, gathers in the bets and walks triumphantly away, leaving a group of astonished suckers who

The whirling Roulette Wheel carries a fascination that is difficult to resist. The players are lured by hope of big winnings, and recklessly stake large amounts.

Facts About Roulette

The Game That Made Monte Carlo Famous—How It Is Played and How the Victims Lose

THE game of roulette is played on a larger scale than any other form of gambling. It has reached its popularity during the seventy-odd years since the establishment of the gambling casino in Monte Carlo and it has supplanted many other games that once were often played.

Roulette is essentially a big money game. It is designed to be played on a large scale and it is built to favor the banker. The players who indulge in this sport are lured by hopes of big return for a small investment, but the gambling house is in it as a purely business proposition. Backed up by the law of averages a roulette wheel will bring a big turnover. Aided by fraud and deception profits can be inflated.

Big Investments Demand Big Profits

Before reading the facts about roulette get this slant on the game. A regulation roulette cannot be started on a shoestring. A full-sized wheel, table and layout costs more than $500 and that is but a part of the investment. Thousands of dollars have been spent in the casino at Monte Carlo making

the place attractive so that wealthy customers will come there. And the same is true in other establishments where roulette is played. Where gambling is illegal profits must be spent in bribing local authorities. The men who put a roulette wheel into operation must be prepared to spend plenty of money. If the game gave the players anything like an even break, these men would be fools to invest in such a precarious venture. Think it over and common sense will tell you that roulette is a good game to keep away from.

How the Game Is Played

The roulette wheel is a circular bowl, raised slightly in the center. The entire center is movable and is mounted upon a shaft which enables it to revolve smoothly and swiftly.

Around the circumference of the wheel, just below the stationary sides of the bowl, is a circle of pockets. There are thirty-eight of these and they are numbered irregularly from 1 to 36, with pockets alternating red and black in color. Beside these pockets there are two special pockets, one marked 0 and the other 00. These are painted green.

The wheel is whirled by the operator and, while it is revolving, he drops a small ball upon it. The ball bounces hither and thither and finally, when the wheel stops, lodges in one of the pockets and indicates the winning number.

With the roulette wheel is a layout, illustrated on this page. The layouts vary in arrangement. The players place their money upon this chart and they have various ways of designating their bets. For example, suppose someone places a dollar upon number 10. As the chances are small that number 10 will attract the ball he will receive thirty-five dollars if he wins.

If the player wishes to increase his chances of getting a winning number, he places his money on the dividing line between two numbers, say 10 and 13. If either 10 or 13 receives the ball, he wins, but he is paid only seventeen dollars for his single dollar bet.

He can place money at the corners of four numbers—say 16, 17, 19 and 20. In this case he receives eight dollars for one if any of the four lucky numbers is the winner.

He can also play the first twelve, second twelve or third twelve numbers on a 2 to 1 basis; or he can play one of the three rows of numbers on the same basis. Thus, if he plays the first twelve and such numbers as 3, 6 or 8 turn up he will win. A glance at the layout shows how the three rows may be played at 2 to 1.

If the player wants to bet on an even basis, he can play the low numbers or the high. For example, if he puts a dollar on the space marked 1 to 18, he will receive his dollar back and another besides if the ball lands in a pocket not over 18. Similarly he may play 19 to 36 inclusive. He may also play odd or even, or red or black on the same basis.

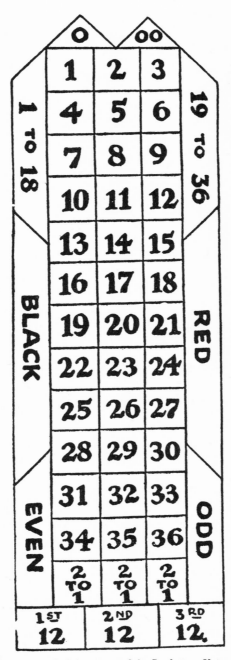

A typical layout used in Roulette. Note the arrangement of the numbers and the various ways in which bets may be placed.

The Odds Favor the Bank

Owing to the presence of numbers 0 and 00 the odds favor the bank, for these numbers are neither odd nor even, red nor black, nor are they between 1 and 36. Whenever one of them turns up the bank sweeps the board. That is called the bank's percentage and, by the law of averages, it represents one spin of the wheel in every nineteen, as there are thirty-eight pockets. That means that about five per cent of the money taken in goes to the bank, everything else being equal.

When big plays are being made the bank is constantly taking in money. Sometimes the heavy play may be on red and the bank may lose by a frequent succession of reds; but, on the other hand, a succession of blacks will help the bank. The five per cent is the bank's big margin.

The Man With a System

Every now and then a man comes along with a "system," which he claims will beat roulette. Some of these fellows have been successful and have made lots of money, but they generally lose it later. A system may be a method of bet play, or it may be used on a faulty wheel which brings up certain numbers more than others. Keen players have discovered faults in wheels before the operators have. But the only way a system will really pay its inventor is when he goes out and sells his idea to some sucker and stays away from the game itself.

When the man with the system gets troublesome the operator will pay special attention to him. The man who runs the wheel knows his business and it is an actual fact that there are operators who can drop the ball on a revolving wheel at just the right instant to keep it from going into a certain pocket.

The one system that may win is when a crooked wheel is used. Then the clever player, by betting his money on colors or numbers that are sparsely covered, will win, for the operator will be keeping the ball away from the big money.

Making Roulette Wheels Crooked

A fair wheel may be made crooked in an instant by means of a little device called the bouncer. This is a wedge of thin, hard rubber that fits into the back of a pocket so closely that it cannot be detected.

Suppose the players are after certain numbers and they are winning regularly. This may just be a peculiar run of luck or the wheel may be slightly out of order. At any rate, one or more numbers are turning up too often.

While he picks the ball up with one hand the skilful operator slips a bouncer into the back of one of the troublesome pockets. From then on the ball will not stay in that pocket, for as it rolls there the rubber will bounce it out again.

Making the Winner Red or Black

Many bets are made on red or black. If most of the players put their money on the red, the operator will, of course, desire black, and vice versa.

For this reason wheels are often fixed so that the operator may produce the desired color.

One method lies in the construction of the strips of metal which make the divisions between the pockets. Each alternate division is slightly longer than the other. If the operator tosses the ball so that it will swing to his right, the result will be black; if he tosses the ball to his left, it will come red.

The most modern device, however, depends upon the use of magnets. The small illustration shows the simplest form. Every other pocket is backed by a small magnet. The operator uses a ball with a steel core when he wants the ball to fall into one of those pockets. The magnet holds the ball as soon as it hesitates on one of those pockets. When the operator does not

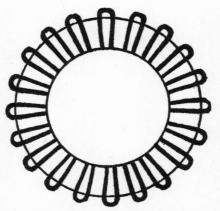

The electrically controlled Roulette Wheel has magnets concealed behind alternate pockets. These attract the ball and throw a percentage to the house.

Double Crossed
Tough Luck for the Bunco Man!

THE bunco man picked up a pack of cards.

"There's a straight deck," he announced. "Take it and shuffle it; mix the cards any way you want. I'll turn my back while you do it. Then when you're ready I'll turn around and cut the pack. The first cut I make will cut the ace of spades! I'll bet you ten dollars I can do it!"

"You're on," replied the quiet man with the polka-dot tie. "Turn your back and let me mix the cards."

Shuffle, shuffle, shuffle.

"All ready," said the man with the polka-dot tie.

The bunco artist turned around and looked at the pack on the table. Then he took a large knife from his pocket, opened the blade, and neatly carved the entire deck of cards in half.

"There's my cut," he announced. "I cut the pack right in half. I cut the ace of spades on the first cut. Pay me the ten-spot!"

"Guess again," replied the quiet man. "You picked the wrong sucker this time. Here's the ace of spades in my pocket. Come across with the mazuma. And the next time you work your little game *don't turn your back!*"

want that particular color he uses another ball that is not magnetized. Then his chances are even and the game is on the square. But the fixed pockets have given him a great advantage over the players.

This method has been elaborated so that different currents may be shot into certain numbers when the operator pushes a switch. The operator knows his business and he turns on the juice whenever advisable. In this way he can knock off the big players until they are out of cash and have to quit.

Detecting Crooked Roulette Wheels

It is only possible to detect crooked wheels by knowledge of methods and careful observation. The bouncers may be seen, if one looks close enough; while if a player wants to investigate a wheel that is magnetized he must either get hold of the ball and apply a magnet to it or hold a small compass near the wheel to see if the presence of magnets influences it.

But even if the player discovers that the wheel is crooked he gains nothing thereby. He will probably get into trouble if he is caught making his tests, and if he gets away with them he simply learns that he had better stay away from that wheel, for trying to play with the operator is a foolish policy. The one way to beat a roulette wheel is to avoid it altogether. It was intended for suckers and it always gets them.

Development of Roulette

Roulette Wheels have spread to such an extent that they are now used throughout the world. Their development has been different from that of any other game. Whereas gambling houses have fitted and adapted ordinary games to suit their needs, the roulette wheel has needed no changes, for it is essentially a game in which the house opposes the player. This fact alone should be remembered by everyone before he tries to beat the game. The best time to quit a proposition like roulette is before you begin.

The Pocket Roulette Wheel

How the Crooked Gamester Trims the Suckers by Simple Methods

POCKET roulette is popular among many gamblers today because it is a quick money getter. When a crowd is ready to bet some money the man who produces one of these contrivances will always have preference over the fellow with a pack of cards or a pair of dice.

The lure of roulette is universal and the game is so easy to understand that anyone can be induced to try it.

In this type of wheel there are only twelve numbers. The bowl is stationary and the whole outfit can be examined. The operator carries a layout in his pocket. He spreads it on the table and spins the ball so that it rolls around inside the bowl.

There is no trick to the little wheel. Everything is fair in construction, but the operation brings the swindle. The man who knows the secret sets the wheel on a table

No special mechanical device is necessary with Pocket Roulette. The diagram shows how the wheel is raised by a dab of wax, thus tilting the bowl in the desired direction.

which is not level and the ball will always end in the lowermost pocket.

All he has to do is to pick the right spot and turn the bowl so that the number he wants is at the bottom of the downward slant and the ball will end there.

If the table is level and will not affect the ball, the operator uses a tiny ball of wax or some other sticky substance. When he sets the wheel on the table he slips the dab of wax underneath one side of the bowl and that side becomes higher.

If a player puts a lot of money on a certain pocket the wax goes under that pocket.

Sometimes two men work this wheel together—one bets and the other throws winning numbers to him. Then it looks as though the operator is going broke and the players spend their money as fast as they can, hoping to be big winners.

But the real winner is the operator, who splits fifty-fifty with his partner after the rest of the crowd have gone.

With the Pocket Roulette is a layout which rolls into small space.

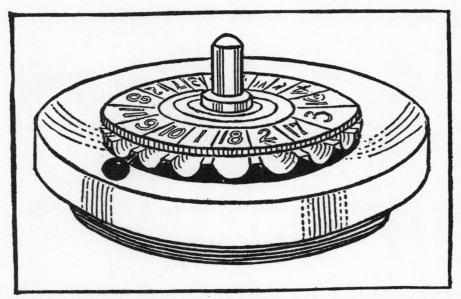

The Miniature Roulette Wheel resembles the regulation apparatus—but it is smaller.

Miniature Roulette

ROULETTE wheels are made in various sizes to satisfy the gamblers who do not want to make a big investment. A small wheel may be set up in a club and it can be removed very quickly. Many of these are sold to private individuals who use them to play roulette in the home instead of indulging in poker or other card games.

The layouts furnished with these wheels are printed on a sheet of cloth, which can be laid down and rolled up very quickly.

Cheap wheels of this type are often inaccurate and spoil the game, as certain numbers turn up too frequently. If the wheels are well made they cost more money. As the man who acts as banker has to put up more money on the game he has the advantage of the 0 and 00, so the percentage is in his favor. In other words, the man who keeps a wheel like this in his home and lets his friends play against him is simply running a small-time gambling joint.

These wheels can be fixed and the higher priced ones are often sold with the crooked apparatus and instructions. There are people who give parties to their friends

and acquaintances and make a nice profit thereby through the use of such roulette wheels.

The explanatory diagram shows the construction of a set roulette wheel which will produce either red or black as desired. This principle is used on large wheels also, but it is specially adapted to smaller wheels that are not large enough for magnets and which cannot be made with electrical connections.

The swindle lies in the partitions between the pockets. Half of these are attached to the outer rim of the wheel, but the others are fixed to the center of the wheel. These divisions are arranged alternately as illustrated. No one can detect the arrangement of the divisions, as they are a close fit.

Below the knob which the operator spins to make the wheel revolve is a tight-fitting clamp which is attached to the center of the wheel. This clamp can be turned the fraction of an inch in either direction. When it is in the center the wheel is fair, but when the operator turns it slightly to the right it narrows the pockets of one color, and the ball will not go into any of those pockets.

When the clamp is turned to the

left the other color is closed. The operator watches the bets and when he sees most of the money on black he shifts the clamp so that the ball is sure to end in a red pocket.

This device can be operated with a minimum of skill and it is impossible to detect the swindle.

Cheap roulette wheels that have no mechanical devices on them often prove disastrous to the owner, for if of faulty construction, players may spot winning numbers.

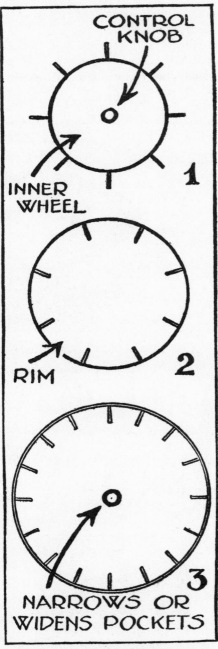

The divisions of the Roulette Wheel are alternately arranged in the manner illustrated. A twist of the central knob closes half the pockets.

Open or shut the closed Roulette Wheel seems fair—yet it is set against the player.

INSIDE of COVER

HOLES OVER POCKETS

SLANTING BOTTOM

Covered Roulette

A Variation of the Famous Game of Monte Carlo — Devised for the Operator and Made to Trim the Victims

HERE is a gambling device that has been built especially for suckers. It is meant to be played as a crooked device and its secret is, therefore, well hidden.

The operator has a roulette wheel which revolves in the usual manner. Besides the wheel there is a metal cover that goes over the wheel but does not cover the numbers which are behind the pockets. The cover, however, hides the pockets themselves.

The wheel is covered and a ball is dropped in an opening at the top of the cover. The apparatus revolves and the ball spins around inside the cover, which has a metal disc beneath it.

In this circular plate are various holes—one for each pocket. The ball, of course, drops through one of the holes and lands in a pocket. When the wheel has ceased to spin the cover is raised and the ball is seen in the pocket where it has fallen.

The Trick Lies in the Cover

Nothing is wrong with the wheel itself. The trick lies in the cover, which will stand close scrutiny. Every hole is exactly the same size and the cover appears to be an innocent contrivance which makes the game absolutely fair, as the operator who drops the ball cannot see the pockets of the wheel and there can be no trickery in the wheel.

The circular plate at the bottom of the cover is not flat, but is humped up in the center. One side of the interior is higher than the other. When the ball is dropped into the cover it naturally rolls to the lower side and then drops through. It can be heard to spin around inside, but the moment the revolution ceases it finds its way to the lower side.

The cover is secretly marked so that the operator can tell the low side from the high. He sets the cover so that the low side comes over a losing hole. Then when he revolves the wheel he has nothing to worry about.

The closed roulette wheel is manufactured with an extra cover that is just what it appears to be. With it the game is played as regular roulette, giving the same chances as a fair roulette wheel. This cover serves two purposes: it may be used in place of the crooked cover while the operator is creating confidence, and it may be substituted for the crooked cover after the players have lost their money.

When one realizes that an outfit of this sort costs close to $150 complete and that it is built to be carried around it is only logical that the game would be crooked. A professional gambler does not invest his money unless he can count on a big return. His life is a precarious one and he wants big profits.

Figure it this way: A gambler buys a roulette wheel. If he plays it fair, he will make an average of five per cent gain on every play. That means he must make the plays come thick and fast, otherwise he'd do better opening a cigar store.

That is why he wants a crooked wheel. It makes a big turnover and increases his profits. If he can win every time, so much the better. He gambles as a business—with the other people it is a form of amusement. He gets the money and they have the fun. That is the way he looks at it and he doesn't lose any sleep crying over the other fellow' hard luck.

Facts and Figures on Punch Boards

PUNCH boards are one of the commonest forms of gambling devices now in use. Although they are barred from many localities, it is an easy matter to keep them out of sight when strangers are around; and in many places they are displayed openly.

These boards are kept in pool rooms, cigar stores, and often drug stores, where they serve as "trade stimulators," the idea being that many customers will spend money in the hope of getting something for nothing. Prizes are paid in trade.

For this reason, the average person supposes that he has an even chance of winning, and he is encouraged in this belief. For example, let us suppose a merchant has a 300-hole punch board, the charge being five cents a punch. The punch board is a "trade stimulator." It will bring in fifteen dollars more quickly than if the storekeeper resorted to straight sales. Therefore he should not object to passing out fifteen dollars' worth of merchandise for fifteen dollars taken in. The board costs him not more than fifty cents, or less than four per cent of fifteen dollars, and he can afford that discount because of the increased trade.

But in actual practice, things work differently. The man who plays punch boards regularly is

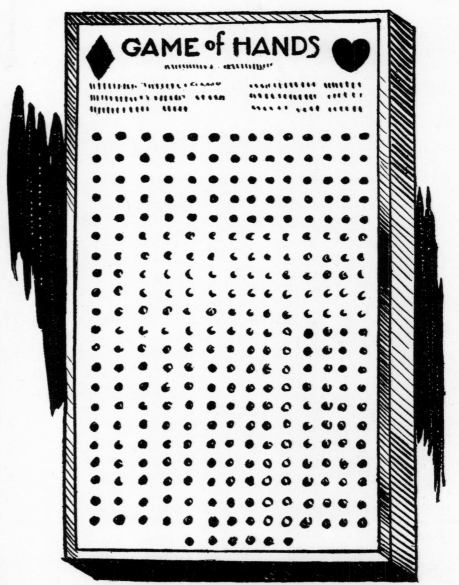

The Poker Board is used as a "trade stimulator" in many stores.

bucking a losing game. The law of averages is against him, and the more he plays, the farther he goes in the hole.

If the reader thinks that a "trade stimulator" gives out full merchandise for the money he takes in, he can go and punch a 300 hole board from beginning to end, and see how he makes out. He will lose $4.50 on the transaction. If he is wise, he will read the figures given here and save himself time and money.

The board costs five cents a punch. The rewards on a poker board are as follows:

Royal flush ...$1.00 in trade
4 of a kind ... .75 in trade
Full house .... .35 in trade
Flush .... .25 in trade
Straights ..... .20 in trade
3 of a kind .... .15 in trade
Two pairs ..... .10 in trade
Any one pair .. .05 in trade
Last Hole Punched Wins $.50 in Trade.

Now note the artful wording of the rewards. The board does not say "full houses" and "flushes"—because there is only one full house and one flush in the board!

The actual rewards, and their total value are given here:

1 Royal flush $1.00
1 4 of a kind........ .75
1 Full house .... .35
1 Flush .... .25
4 Straights.......... .80
9 Threes............ 1.35
20 Two pairs........ 2.00
70 Pairs 3.50
Last hole .... .50
———
Total $10.50

The owner of the board stimulates his trade, sometimes to the point of doubling or tripling his sales, and he gets $4.50, in addition. Deducting the $.50 for the cost of the board, his excess profits total $4.00

Now let's look at it from the player's standpoint. He is out to win. The 70 holes that pay 5 cents are "dead heads"—that is, they

neither win nor lose as far as he is concerned, although they give the merchant profit on a five cent sale.

For the player, there are just 37 winning holes out of 230. He and his playmates can spend $11.50, and they can win only $7.00. That means their chances are less than two against three—not even money. The reward on the last hole induces players to punch until the board is finished.

Sometimes, players refuse to punch a board after the big prizes have been "knocked off." When the storekeeper runs a board in this way, among a regular group of players, he is then entering into the gamble himself, and he will often fail to make his $4.50 excess profit—except when the big prizes hold out to the end. Still the odds are slightly in his favor.

To offset this, there are board men who use marked boards. When they buy the board, a slip of paper comes with it saying "5-7," or some such number. The storekeeper counts five holes across, and seven down. He punches that

hole himself, at the first opportunity, and out pops the royal flush. That means one dollar in the storekeeper's pocket, and the odds are increased against the players.

In discussing the poker board, we have considered the most generous of them all. In other boards the odds are much greater against the player. Some boards have 3000 or 4000 holes, and a large assortment of prizes is offered, amounting to nearly $100. But when we realize that the boards take in from $300 to $400 if they are played to the end, we see that the odds can be more than 3 to 1 against the players!

One of the latest punch boards has five colors, black giving one to one; red, two to one; green, five to one; blue, ten to one; and white, twenty to one. If the player bets a dime on blue, and punches a blue ticket, he gets one dollar. This looks big to the player. A bet on white and a lucky punch brings him twenty times what he paid!

This is the most deceptive of all boards, and is a great money maker for the owner. Most of the tickets are black—paying one to one—and of course no one plays the black. A man may bet on white and punch a blue ticket. He gets nothing. The percentage of white, blue, green, and red tickets is amazingly small compared to the number of black ones. If a group of players would stick to one color all the way through the storekeeper would be the big winner. Only a remarkable succession of lucky guesses can break down his profits, and even then the black tickets will save him from loss. On the other hand, poor guesses will increase his profits, and he may take in $120 on a 1200 hole board without paying out more than $10 or $15.

These boards are sold for about $1.50, and the storekeepers get big returns for their money. Furthermore the color boards are good right to the last hole—that is, good for the owner, but tough for the player!

The Alluring Slot Machines

Mechanical Devices That Reap a Mighty Harvest of Unearned Dollars

THERE are thirty or forty different makes of gambling slot machines in existence. A classification of them would read like a catalog. They are set strong against the players and their construction is all in favor of the owner.

The slot machines that get the biggest play are those which take a nickel. The player drops the coin in a slot, pulls a handle and wheels revolve. In stopping they form different combinations which pay the player various sums—and sometimes nothing.

The machines that are most popular deliver the money automatically. Sometimes they are played with checks or slugs which the player trades in for cash.

There is no need to go into the details of the mechanism of the usual nickel slot machine. It has supplanted many of the other machines and its mechanical operation and the percentages on the wheel favor the owner of the machine to an enormous degree. A man will buy a hundred-dollar machine and run it in violation of the law. If he gets away with it for a few weeks he doesn't worry if the machine is grabbed. He will have a big profit and enough over to buy a new machine.

Three aces give the player fifteen cents in return for five. But winning combinations are few and far between.

<table>
<tr><td colspan="2" align="center">TABLE OF PRIZES</td></tr>
<tr><td>Royal Flush—pays ....</td><td>$5.00</td></tr>
<tr><td>(Ace, king, queen, jack and ten of one suit.)</td><td></td></tr>
<tr><td>Straight Flush ....</td><td>2.50</td></tr>
<tr><td>(All of one suit in rotation.)</td><td></td></tr>
<tr><td>Four of a Kind ....</td><td>1.00</td></tr>
<tr><td>Full House ....</td><td>.50</td></tr>
<tr><td>Flush (all of one suit) ....</td><td>.30</td></tr>
<tr><td>Straight (all in rotation) ....</td><td>.25</td></tr>
<tr><td>Three of a Kind ....</td><td>.15</td></tr>
<tr><td>Two Pair ....</td><td>.10</td></tr>
<tr><td>One Pair (jacks or better) ....</td><td>.05</td></tr>
</table>

Slot machines are the most ingenious of mechanical gambling devices. The player cannot see the interior and he plays it blindly. Why men of common sense will fritter away their cash on games like these is hard to tell. The more they play the more they lose.

When you play a slot machine the odds are not only against you, but the machine probably has much more money in it than you have in your pocket. A loss of twenty dollars may break the player, but it would take much more than that to break the machine and then the owner would put in more money. Once the machine gets ahead of the game it is finis for the player. He is bucking a game that has been devised to trim him.

Small Chances of Winning

About the only way to play a slot machine with anything like an even break is to start with a sum of about two dollars. If that is lost, quit. On the other hand, if the player should get well ahead of the game, he should pocket everything he wins, always keeping exactly two dollars to play with. As soon as he drops that two dollars he should quit—then he may walk out with some winnings. He can reduce the amount of playing margin from two dollars to one if he wishes as he gets ahead of the game.

But remember, this is not a method to beat a slot machine. There is no system that will bring results. A player may win a few dollars at the most. He is foolish even to play the game. The average person loses his head when he gets ahead of the game and won't quit. Once he is behind he keeps on playing to regain his losses. Plenty of pay envelopes have been emptied into slot machines. They are the greatest form of sucker bait ever invented.

A Look Inside a Slot Machine

If a player could study the dial of the regular slot machine he would gain some enlightenment. For this reason an illustration is given exposing the poker slot machine—which is the worst offender of them all. It actually takes money under false pretenses.

The machine is illustrated here. It has five revolving wheels, each bearing different playing cards. As every gambler knows the game of poker it is easy to get players in this game. The rewards in the game are often cigars, but sometimes money is given. The chart at the top of the page serves as an example.

This looks good to the player and he will squander his money in hopes of connecting with a royal flush or a straight flush. But he is wasting his efforts, and if he thought matters over a bit he would see why.

In the first place, the player is misled. He thinks he is working on a straight poker basis with a chance of any possible combination. Now naturally the machine would not be made so that two identical cards would appear at once—on different wheels. There are just fifty-two cards in a pack, and these must be distributed

among five wheels—that is, about ten different cards to each wheel.

The picture with the rows of cards shows how this can be done. Each vertical row represents a different wheel. It will be noted that,

Poker Slot Machine. Each vertical row is curved to form a wheel. Study the arrangement of the cards, and you will see that many of the large winning combinations are impossible to attain. Straight Flushes are eliminated—and only one Four of a Kind can possibly appear.

while cards are duplicated on the same wheel, no card appears on more than one wheel

Not a Chance for a Big Prize

Every time a nickel is dropped in the slot the wheels spin. One card appears from each wheel. Now where are the chances for a royal flush? There aren't any! Look at the layout of cards and you will see that two cards of one suit, such as a queen and a jack, appear on the same wheel. Goodbye, royal flush!

Look for a straight flush. You will find that it is also impossible with this layout. Where are the four aces? Two different aces appear on one wheel. That eliminates four aces. Most of the possible combinations of four of a kind are completely out of the picture, although it is possible.

Full houses are hard to make, and flushes are not easy. Look at spades, for example. The ace is the only spade on one wheel. In order to make a flush in spades that one particular card must appear. The possibilities of a flush in any other suit are also limited.

The player has a chance for some of the small prizes, but the percentage is greatly against him. He would be wise enough not to risk his money for the little prizes. What he is after is the big rewards, *which he can never get.*

As the mechanism is not on view the unthinking player does not realize what he is up against. During the course of many plays he will see practically every card in the pack. He will not note which wheel each one is on and he will think the machine is a fair one.

Slot Machines Are All Alike

As regards their effect on the player, all slot machines are alike. Every one is a tough baby to beat. Some of the larger machines, with six slots, are plugged on certain slots so that winning is impossible. Others have mechanical devices that help to rob the player. Yet the suckers keep on coming.

In order to make these machines

legal they are often introduced as vending machines. Along side of each machine is a container that delivers packages of mints—a package for each nickel. The candy resembles regular five-cent packages, but it is of a cheap grade. The man who owns the machine can let the mints go—his profits are big enough. This should convince some of the suckers that they are in wrong, but it doesn't.

Players seldom pay any attention to the mints as they are after money—not candy. So the latest model machines deliver mints on every play automatically, to prove that they are not gambling devices. The players get plenty of candy and the machines take in the money. If you try to beat one of these machines, carry a suitcase. All you will get is candy and you might as well bring it home as a souvenir.

Telling the Winner Beforehand

The cleverest improvement on the nickel slot machine was the device which told the player what he was going to win! This was done to prove that the machine was not a gambling device. Every time a nickel was dropped in the slot

---

Phoney Advertisements

THE person who invented this one evidently had a sense of humor.

EXTERMINATE INSECTS

Flies, potato bugs, ants and all other insects can be killed instantly with our special apparatus. No powder, spray, or poison. Simple instructions explain everything. Price, $1.00.

URA SAP, Tenafter, Tenn.

The person who sends a dollar gets something for his money—in the shape of a tiny block and mallet. Accompanying the apparatus are brief directions which tell him to catch the bugs or insects and lay them on the block and then hit them with the mallet. This, if properly done, will mean sure death!

---

the wheels spun, winning or losing combinations turned up and a number appeared in a small hole telling just how many nickels the player would get *on the next play.*

Naturally, when a player approached the machine he would see the figure 0 showing, which would mean that he would lose his nickel. But what he wanted to see was the *next* number, which might be a winner. So he would waste his first nickel. Every time 0 would show up he would take another chance. If a number like 5 (meaning five nickels or twenty-five cents) would appear, he would lose no time in getting after it.

Just think this over. When a machine can be so constructed that it will tell the number that is going to appear before a nickel is dropped in, should any sane person believe that machine to be on the level? If it can tell one ahead, why not two, three, four, five or any number of successive plays? Yet these slot machines, which were legal in certain localities, did the biggest business in the history of the game. All of which proves that when Barnum said "There is one born every minute" he made a very conservative estimate.

Manipulating Machines

Sometimes a man who knows the game can manipulate the slot machine so as to make it deliver without putting in a coin. Other players put in slugs and take out nickels. Where machines must be kept under cover, the proprietor stays outside to keep watch, and if a clever player gets alone with the machine, he can make it pay. If the handles are pulled down to a certain point, and a coin is dropped in, the machines will sometimes repeat. It is possible to put a machine out of order; and sometimes their mechanism becomes faulty. Then the lucky player who has nerve and opportunity will take his toll from the contrivance. But this is not a frequent occurrence. As a rule, the owners are the boys who get the coin.

The player rolls the dice on the cigar counter. If he is lucky he may win something.

Cigar Counter Dice Games
How They Stimulate Trade and Fleece the Sucker

GAMES of counter dice are very popular, and whenever they are permitted they do a big business. This is true of certain hotels and other establishments in the Middle West. The game is played on the cigar counter, and prizes are given in trade.

There are various ways of playing the game. For example, a player may roll ten dice from a box. Before he begins, he chooses a number, like 5; or he can take two numbers, as 5 and 6. He pays a quarter for the privilege of choosing a number.

He rolls the dice ten times, and each time the man behind the counter records the number of times the player's point appears. Suppose the player's point is 5. It may appear three times the first roll; twice the second; once the third; four times the fourth. The cigar man adds them up.

If the player's point appears 20 times in the course of ten rolls, he gets 50 cents in trade. If it appears 25 times, he gets $1.00 in trade; if it shows up 30 times, he gets $2.00.

Now there are six sides to every dice. If twelve dice were used, the player's number would appear 20 times in ten rolls. But with ten dice, his average should be between 16 and 17.

That is where the store makes its margin of profit. In the long run, most players will lose the quarter they put up. The cigar stand can afford to pay to the winners.

In checking up on one of these games, it was found that a lucky player, who had some real breaks, won about thirteen dollars after playing ten dollars on the counter. In other words, he got thirteen dollars' worth of merchandise for ten dollars in cash. The store could afford it, for the player was forced to take a lot of cigars and cigarettes, and the stand operated on a good margin of profit. In the meantime, other players were spending three, four, or five dollars, and getting from 50 cents to one dollar in return.

The above has been given simply as an example; there are so many different ways of counting up scores that it is difficult to trace them all. Sometimes the player rolls eight dice for a dime, and gets his reward in cigars. Only totals like 8 or 48 pay big prizes; numbers 9, 10, 11, 12 pay good prizes, as do 44, 45, 46, 47; but the middle numbers from 20 to 36 pay either one cigar or nothing. The great majority of the totals fall between 20 and 36. The game pays a good profit to the operator. Rolling eight aces or eight sixes may not sound very difficult, but those combinations show up about once in ten years.

In some of these games, the operator puts up bigger rewards, and makes it look possible for the player to win plenty, because the odds are lessened against him; in fact, they may be in his favor. Whenever you encounter a game of that type it is a safe bet that it is crooked.

A concealed magnet beneath the counter gives the operator the big advantage, and the player never wins.

How the Dice Are Loaded

In the first place, when a lot of dice are used, it is an easy matter for the man behind the counter to ring in one or two loaded dice. In fact, they can be in the game most of the time. Some players go after a certain number in the combination games and stick to it. If one of the dice is loaded against the player his chances are considerably lessened.

But the most common method is to use electric dice. The dice are solid ones, and three sides, say the low ones—1, 2, 3—have lead beneath them. The other sides—4, 5, 6—are made with a thin facing of iron.

Under the counter is a magnet device, as illustrated, with a switch-button. Now when the electromagnet is not in use, the high numbers will show up most frequently. If the player is after 1, 2, or 3, the gamester lets nature take its course. The heavy lead sides of the dice make the high numbers predominate, as 1, 2, and 3 come beneath.

As soon as a player goes after 4, 5, or 6, the operator presses the button or the switch, and the magnet beneath the counter makes the high sides come down, so that most of the numbers are 1, 2, and 3.

The ordinary magnet is simply placed under a solid counter. But when a glass show-case is used, the magnet is camouflaged in what appears to be a humidor, used to keep cigars fresh. This is just beneath the glass surface of the counter, and it is innocent in appearance; but it does the trick every time.

Concealing Electro-Magnet

Sometimes the magnet is hidden in a sort of cash box, which rests on the counter and serves as a pedestal on which the dice are rolled. The concealment of the magnet is a simple matter, and anyone can handle the switch with ease.

In other games, the dice roll into a bowl, which is fitted up electrically. Here, again all the chances are against the player; the concealed switch does it all.

Tables are made for rolling dice; and electro-magnets in the table top control the special electric dice. The wires run up the big central table leg, and the switch may be out of the room. Such devices are used in gambling houses.

A confederate handles the button to help the gambler who is swindling the other players, in any kind of dice game they may choose.

Electric Transparent Dice

Elsewhere in this book, the loading of transparent dice is explained. The use of platinum in the spots is the method. To make transparent dice respond to a hidden magnet, the spots are also hollowed out and soft iron is inserted. Then the spots are repainted, and the dice are ready for use.

It is the best to stay away from all counter games or elaborate dice games where the player tries to beat the bank; for it is a sure thing that the odds of the game are naturally against the player, or that some secret contrivance is working in favor of the house. Generally the electro-magnet is the hidden device; and even the wisest cannot find it.

Matching Coins

THERE are various unfair methods of matching coins employed by bunco artists. Double-headed or double-tailed coins are not unknown to these people and they do not hesitate to use such artifices.

Another type of coin is made to fall heads every time it is twirled on the table. Anyone may spin the coin, but the result will always be the same.

This is because the edge of the coin is filed at an angle, so that it is not straight. The edge has a greater diameter at the head side than at the tail.

When the coin is twirling it naturally leans, and as the spin begins to diminish the coin falls with the tail down and registers heads.

Such coins are difficult to detect as the angle of the edge is very slight—yet sufficient enough to assure the same result every time.

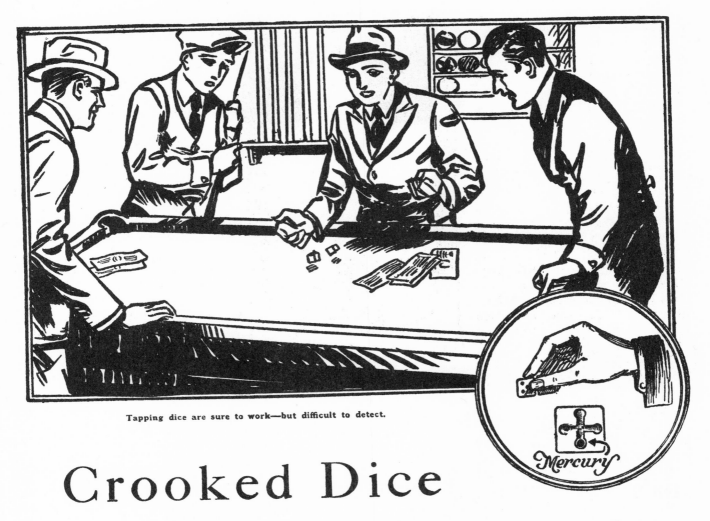

Tapping dice are sure to work—but difficult to detect.

Crooked Dice

Exposing the Methods of Unfair Gamblers—Protecting the Public Against Swindlers

GAMBLING with dice is an old, old story, and it has reached its modern development in the game of craps, which is said to have originated among ignorant natives of South America.

It is doubtful if any game could be more simple in theory than craps. The player takes the dice and bets a certain amount of money, which is covered by another player. If he rolls 7 or 11, he wins the stakes; if he rolls 2, 3 or 12, he loses. If he rolls another point—say 6—he must keep on rolling until he repeats that number, when he wins; but if he should roll 7 before his 6, he loses, and the privilege of rolling goes to another person.

Loaded Dice

Everyone knows that dice can be loaded. The first crooked dice were crude, as they were weighted on the bottoms and would show the same number so often that players would become suspicious. This led to the invention of dice that would roll any desired number.

These dice have a hollow chamber under each side. All the chambers are connected and one chamber contains mercury.

The player simply holds the dice with the desired sides up. Then he taps the dice before he rolls them. The mercury drops into the bottom chambers and the dice roll just as the player wants them. Another tap changes the numbers.

These are loaded dice, but the load shifts and few people suspect them. (See illustration.)

Loaded Transparent Dice

In order to make loading of dice impossible transparent dice were manufactured. They are made of a material that people can see through, so, of course, the dice can't be loaded—presumably!

As a matter of fact, transparent dice are often loaded. This is done by boring out the spots on the underneath sides to the depth of a fraction of an inch and filling the small cavities with platinum, one of the heaviest of all metals. Then the spots are painted on again and the result is a pair of dice that will stand the closest inspection, yet which will often roll the desired number. This gives the player a good percentage.

As platinum is very expensive some dice are filled with gold or other heavy metal, but platinum is most effective.

How to Detect Loaded Dice

No matter how cleverly dice are loaded they can generally be detected. The best system is to drop them into a glass of water. As they sink to the bottom they will turn with the loaded sides down. Several tests will tell the story. If a die is held by opposite corners between the thumb and forefinger, a loaded side will often make it turn to the bottom.

Capped Dice

An expensive method of loading dice is to cut off one side of each die and attach a new face made of a transparent material which is heavier than the ordinary substance used. This can be done so perfectly that no one will detect it. The dice are not filled on the spots so they can stand the closest inspection, and even if they are cut apart no trace will be seen. Certain dice have been manufactured in which one side is made heavier under pressure. It is impossible to detect these dice except by the glass of water test, and even then it is difficult, as the weighted side is only slightly heavier, being intended to give a winning percentage during a long game.

Dice Liquids

Certain liquids have been advertised and it is claimed that when they are applied to the faces of dice they will make a change in the composition of the celluloid, causing the desired sides to become heavier. These liquids have often been over-rated.

Many players simply use collodion, a colorless liquid which they paint on sides of the dice. This liquid cannot be noticed, but when

A mechanical dice box enables the gambler to exchange loaded dice for true ones quickly and indetectibly.

the dice are held in the closed hand the heat makes the painted sides sticky. Then the sharper rolls them on a rug or a pool table and the collodion makes the painted sides stop when they come in contact with the cloth. These dice also give a good percentage in favor of the operator.

Mis-spotted Dice

When a pair of dice is on the table only three sides can be seen at one time. Someone discovered that fact years ago and invented mis-spotted dice.

Originally one of the dice was made with just three numbers, 1, 3 and 5, while the other had only 3, 4 and 5. The two aces were on opposite sides; also the two threes and the two fives, so that no one could see two identical numbers at once.

Study these numbers: 1-3-5; 3-4-5. You will see that such a pair of dice can roll only 4, 5, 6, 8, 9, 10 and 11. Thus the player cannot make a craps (2, 3 or 12), but he can make a natural (11). If

he rolls any other number he is bound to win the point, for 7 is impossible with these dice so he will get the point he wants before he makes the impossible 7.

The trouble with such dice is that 1 and 6 are on adjacent sides, which is not correct and it may be detected. So newer styles have come into use.

In each set both dice are alike. They have the numbers 1, 3 and 5. As people can see no more than three sides these dice look fair. The player can only roll 2, 4, 6, 8 or 10. He may lose on a crap (2), but he will retain the dice, and whenever he rolls 4, 6, 8 or 10 it is sure to turn up again and win for him, as no 7 is possible.

Another combination has dice with numbers 2, 4 and 6 on each dice. These will roll 4, 6, 8, 10 and 12, but no 7. There is danger of rolling 12, but the odds are all in favor of the player.

A third combination uses numbers 2, 3 and 6—again these dice look fair; 4, 5, 6, 8, 9 and 12 may be rolled with these dice—but no 7 will turn up.

Switching Dice

If the dice just mentioned should get into the hands of a player other than the crooked gambler, the party would be over. For that reason it is necessary to switch them for genuine dice. This can be done by using the trick dice box illustrated on this page. It has one compartment for loaded or mis-spotted dice and the other for genuine dice. A flap can be made to cover either bottom compartment at will, so the crooked player can roll either fair dice or otherwise. He also has an unprepared dice box on hand.

But most players do not use the box. They hold the crooked dice in the bent fingers of the right hand and pick up the fair dice with the left. In transferring the fair dice from left hand to right they are retained in the left hand and the crooked dice are shaken in the right. This is very deceptive and can be done with great cleverness.

Loaded dice may be introduced into the game and left there, but mis-spots must be switched in and out, so they are generally used only by the "man behind the table" in a gambling house.

Special Belts for Loaded Dice

Some gamblers wear special belts with pockets for all types of loaded dice. They can obtain the crooked dice at a moment's notice and they pick dice that match the ordinary ones in play. Then they switch in their own dice and win.

Shaped Dice

Shaped dice are slightly lop-sided, having one side shaved so that they are not perfect cubes. One side of each dice is larger than the opposite side and the dice have a marked tendency to come to rest upon the large sides.

The shaping is often done in manufacture and it requires good workmanship, otherwise the dice will not look right. To detect shaped dice square them up, placing two side by side in different positions and the taper of the dice will become noticeable.

Some dice are made in combination of shapes and loads. That is, the dice are loaded very slightly and are also shaped very slightly. This makes it difficult to detect that they are either shaped or loaded; yet the two work in combination and produce results.

In using shaped dice the players do not expect quick profit. They count on a noticeable percentage in their favor.

Operating Crooked Dice

There are various combinations used in loading or shaping dice, and experienced gamblers play for percentage. They do not seek to win all the time, but merely to throw the advantage in their favor.

Loaded dice can be fixed so that one, two or three sides of a dice are loaded. This allows numerous combinations which are used for various purposes. Here are some examples:

Passers

One die is loaded to bring up up 3, 5 or 6; the other to produce 3 or 5. Result: Numbers 6, 8, 9, 10 and 11 show up very frequently. Player has a chance to make 11 on his first throw, but no 7 or craps. If he misses 11, he will generally make his point (6, 8, 9 or 10) before the 7 appears.

Passers

One dice is loaded to bring up 2 or 4; the other to bring up 2 or 6. Result: Numbers 4, 6, 8 and 10 show up most frequently.

Missouts

One die is loaded to produce 1 and 5; the other 1 and 2. Result: 2 and 3 show up often, while 7 is frequent. The player will lose by making many craps. Occasionally he will roll 7 and win; but when he rolls any other number, 7 will usually appear before he makes his point. These dice are employed by the banker so the players will lose.

Missouts

Only one of the dice is loaded. It comes up 1 or 2 most of the time. This brings up 2 and 3 quite often, and slows up the appearance of 7. Again the player loses to the banker.

Above are but a few of the examples. As any one, two, or three sides may be loaded, provided they are not opposites (1-6; 2-5; 3-4) all sorts of combinations may be formed, especially when only one die may be loaded and the other ordinary.

Improved Shaped Dice

With shaped dice, various combinations are also possible. The most improved shaped dice have all sides slightly convex, or rounded, except the opposite sides. For example, the only really flat sides are the 1 and 6, which are opposites. Result: the player will roll 2, 7 and 12 quite often. His chances of craps or a 7 are even; but when he throws another point

on his first roll he is generally sunk, because the 7 is sure to pop up very quickly. Thus the percentage is against the man who has the dice.

A player using these dice will get in a large crap game and cover as many bets as possible while others are rolling the dice. When he gets the cubes himself, he will be careful how he bets. If he has the biggest roll among the players, he will be able to cover many bets and will win consistently throughout the game. When a banker has these dice, and all bets are made against him, he is in the winning position.

Space does not permit a discussion of various other combinations, but they are not necessary, for this information is not for the would-be cheater. He gets all the dope he wants by paying for it, which he does not hesitate to do, as he expects to get a big return for the money he invests.

On the other hand, it will help the fellow who always plays fair, and it is hoped that he will have enough sense to keep away from crap games in the future. Very few suckers realize that dice are made to work against them when they themselves are rolling. They watch the other players with suspicion, but think that everything is sure to be right when they have the dice in their own possession. Such, however, is not the case. A man often loses more quickly when he is rolling the dice himself, and missouts are very popular dice among crooked gamblers.

Crooked dice are easy to get; they are manufactured by thousands, and they are introduced into many friendly games. Some suckers are carrying crooked dice around with them without knowing it—dice which have been switched and planted on them by sharpers, so that when the player uses his own dice in the nightly crap game, the sharper will win. All dice should be tested, but the best way to be safe is to avoid the game.

Marked Cards

Secret Systems Exposed—
How Cards Are Marked in Play

Each card is marked for suit and value. The marks are made by hand on standard backs.

The card shown above is unmarked. It is the two of diamonds.

Compare it with the marked cards at the left. Braces on the bicycles indicate values —ace, king, queen, etc.

Suits other than diamonds are shown either by a heavy line near the border of the fan, or by a tiny brace beneath the saddle of the bicycle.

MARKED cards have been in use for hundreds of years—probably ever since gambling with cards was first originated. Thousands of people are swindled today by sharpers who use marked cards, for it is one of the commonest methods of crooked gambling.

Any card player who is willing to cheat his friends immediately thinks of using marked cards. He has no skill, and he wants to gain an advantage. Marked cards are cheap and plentiful—if he knows where to get them—and once he has obtained a marked pack he is ready to start his crooked career.

Experienced gamesters combine marked cards with skill; but any dub can flounder along and win consistently if he knows how to read a marked pack. That is why so many of them are sold.

Most marked packs have standard backs; they are marked by hand, generally before the game, but sometimes during the play. Of course it takes a slick worker to mark the other man's pack during the game. The vast majority of marked packs are prepared beforehand and are slipped into a game where the victim will not suspect them.

Samples of marked cards are illustrated here. Every style of back can be marked and probably has been. It would be impossible to illustrate all these backs with complete systems of marking on every card. The reader could not begin to remember them. Furthermore, the purpose of this book is to expose and to counteract crooked gambling—not to encourage it. To explain systems of marking an entire deck might tempt someone to try it. If a person plays fair, he is entitled to protection against

sharpers. On a following page he will find the secret of detecting marked cards, and that is what he really needs to know. It is a system that will save a person hundreds of dollars if he plays cards with strangers, and no person should ever fail to make use of it.

First let us explain how cards are marked to show what dangerous weapons they are in the hands of a sharper who is swindling an innocent victim. There are several methods of doctoring a standard deck. This work is done by hand with a pen and ink of proper color.

Block Out

This consists in "blocking out" certain white dots or ornaments that appear on the normal back of the card. If there are several ornaments, they are "blocked out" in accordance with a system which cannot be noticed even when a card is compared with another—unless you know just where to look. For example, the white wheel of a carriage may have a different quarter or half "blocked out." The marks are quite plain to those who know them.

Bracing

When a design has various straight lines in it all the marker has to do is add extra lines at proper places. These cards are easy to read, but hard to detect.

Line Marks

Similar to bracing, but used on packs where short lines can be introduced into the design. A line may be made heavier, bringing it into greater prominence.

Shading

Here a design is taken where a white or slightly shaded ornament appears, such as an angel with wings. Different parts of the ornament are shaded very neatly, so that they appear darker than the others. A different combination is used on each card.

Detecting Marked Cards

It is hardly necessary to remark that the victim is up against a powerful system when he bucks marked cards. Much ingenuity has been put into making them and the work is indeed difficult to detect. Yet there is one simple weapon which offsets the work of the card markers and anyone can employ it without difficulty.

That weapon is the riffle. It has enabled plenty of players to ruin the best laid plans of swindlers. It is illustrated here and its employment is simple but practical.

The man who suspects marked cards simply holds the pack in his left hand and riffles it with his right fingers, so that the cards fall in rapid succession. While doing this he keeps his eyes upon the backs of the cards.

If the pack is marked, he will immediately detect it, for he will see a series of "moving pictures." The marked portion of the design will be different on each card and they will jump around in all directions. For example, if a pack is braced, the brace line will turn from one position to another. If a little angel is shaded, the darkened section will jump from head to wing, to arm and back to the other wing in an amazing manner. If parts of a small carriage wheel are blocked out, the wheel will appear to revolve. It is just like the old "moving-picture book" that were sold ten or fifteen years ago. The difference between two pictures was unnoticeable, but when a book of them was riffled the result was apparent motion.

By use of this system a marked pack loses its poison fangs. One crooked gambler will not use a marked deck against another, for the dupe will simply riffle the pack, find that it is marked, and then study the system to use it for himself!

Cards Marked in Play

Marking cards in play is a common practice of certain gamblers, who get away with it because the victims do not suspect their own packs. The gambler uses a little device which enables him to dab the margins of the cards with tiny spots in accordance with a simple system which is illustrated here. Some of them use a red dabber for red backs and a blue dabber for blue backs; but a green dabber will do for both colors.

Other crooked gamesters nick the edges of the cards with their thumbnails. In this manner they can utilize the same system, but usually they apply it only to cer-

The dabber is a tiny device which enables the gambler to mark the cards during play.

tain cards, such as the aces and kings or cards of a certain suit. It is not necessary to mark an entire pack, for a partly marked deck will give a good percentage.

Luminous Marks

One of the most dangerous systems of marking is with luminous paint, which is visible only in the dark. In order to see the marks the gambler wears a pair of dark

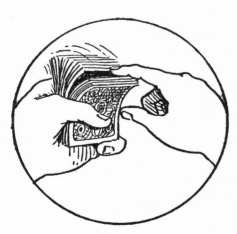

How to detect Marked Cards. This is the surest method. Simply riffle the pack and watch for the "moving pictures."

Cards marked by the dabber are done in the combination shown. No end mark means spades—no side mark a two spot.

glasses. · While this system was known to a very few it was effective, but now anyone who has heard of it will simply ask the gambler to take off his glasses and thus finish his little game.

White Backed Cards

Sometimes players use packs which have perfectly white backs. These can be marked by nicking the edges, but dabs or other marks will soon show up. The usual system on such packs is to glaze the backs with a small piece of wax. Horizontal, vertical and diagonal lines form a simple system, and they are not visible under ordinary light. The crooked gambler

By nicking the edges of certain cards the gambler is able to keep track of them after the pack has been shuffled.

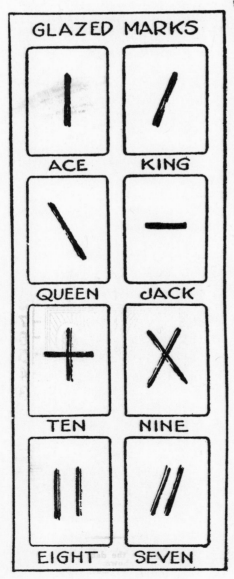

GLAZED MARKS

ACE   KING

QUEEN   JACK

TEN   NINE

EIGHT   SEVEN

sits in a position where the light falls at the proper angle and he can see the marks while other people cannot.

This same system is also applied to cards that have a plain design on the back. The glaze will show up well in the correct light, but only an accident will enable the victim to notice it.

Where Marked Cards Fail

As stated before the veteran gambler will often use a marked pack to his own advantage when he discovers that it has been marked. But he must know the game to do this—it is simply a case of a crook catching a crook, and if the man who makes the discovery can cheat better than his opponent, he will win. A fair player, who would attempt such a thing, would be lowering himself to the level of the crook, and he would probably lose for he would be trying to beat a man at his own game.

If a player suspects that marked cards are used against him, he should make sure of it by using the riffle system or watching for other tricks of the gamester. Then he

should quit the game or show up the crook.

Above all no person should allow himself to be cajoled into using marked cards. Two gamblers will often work a frame-up. One will supply the victim with marked cards and show him how easy it is to cheat. Then the other gambler will pose as a sucker. He knows the marks and a lot of other things beside. The victim will be double-crossed and will lose instead of winning. He can raise no protest, for the marked cards are his own, and in the showdown he will lose his money and be branded as a cheat, while the gambler fattens his bankroll and feigns injured innocence.

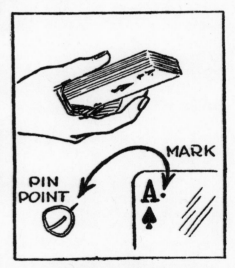

A tiny pin point near the corner of a certain card enables the gambler to recognize the card when he deals it. A tiny device with a pin point is used to prick the cards early in the game. Later the gambler uses them to his own advantage.

Skill With Marked Cards

Experienced players who use marked cards do not rely upon the cards alone. They combine skill in dealing to trim the sucker. In a game like Black Jack or Red Dog the gambler, in dealing, watches for a desirable card on top of the pack. When it appears he keeps it there by tricky dealing, saving it for himself. In such games cards are marked for value only—not for suit. Hand-marked cards are sold without suit marks. These are only added upon request.

Cards Marked in Manufacture

The Story of a Master Pack That Won Thousands of Dollars Before Its Secret Was Discovered

FOR many years playing cards have been manufactured with marked backs. This is done by using a different plate for each back and having a systematic arrangement of marks on the back.

At one time many gamblers used these cards—but that was years ago. The playing-card industry reached a high state and no reputable manufacturer will print marked cards today.

The printing of such cards was carried on by fly-by-night concerns and their cards became so cheap and had such strange backs that gamblers could spot them immediately and were too wise to play with them. Hand-marked packs, on regulation backs, were far more suitable to the needs of gamesters.

Today there are several types of cards that are marked in manufacture, but they are made for the use of magicians. They have clock-like designs that enable a person to read the backs at a considerable distance and some of them have an elaborate system of marking that can be used in tricks but not in games.

While these cards are not sold for gambling purposes they are sometimes used that way, but no man who has any brains would be duped by them, for the backs of these cards are unlike any regulation pack and the system can be learned in a few minutes at the card table. Manufactured marked backs were out of date among American gamblers thirty years ago, but they were used in Europe at a later date, and therein lies a tale—the story of a gigantic swindle with marked cards.

Master Marks

An American invented a pack of

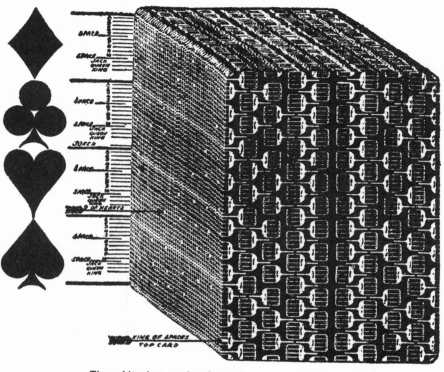

Tiny white dots on the edges tell every card in the pack!

cards that seemed to have no possible use in gambling. These cards were *marked on the edge*. The marks were so small that even the person who knew them could not see the mark on any individual card!

What then was the use of such a pack?

Look at the large illustration and you will see!

When the entire pack was squared up and then spread slightly the tiny marks would appear—white dots on red lines—that stood out like signals. They were invisible when the pack was squared up, and also when it was spread too wide; but when the pack was slightly spread out the points would show up amazingly.

This pack was made for magicians. With it a performer could let anyone shuffle the pack, which had a semi-regulation pattern on

the back. Nothing suspicious about the cards. They could be examined closely, but when the performer took the pack in his own hands and spread it slightly he could instantly cut to any card in the pack by looking for the white signals!

This amazing pack of cards sprang into immediate popularity; then it suddenly disappeared from the market and none of the cards can be bought today. Here is the story as told by a man who was in a position to know.

It appears that a purchaser from Europe arranged to buy a large quantity of these cards, stating that they were for novelty dealers. He specified that the ace of spades should be of peculiar design, showing a skull and crossbones over a scimitar. This was a startling pattern, so it was used on all the cards thereafter.

Big Swindle

These cards were sent to Europe and were really intended for a clique of gamblers. They sold the cards at a low price so that they were bought by large gambling houses on the continent. The backs looked all right and the marks could not be detected, so the cards were accepted.

This is the mysterious design which was ordered for the ace of spades. Its sinister appearance spelled the doom of those who played against it.

Then the big swindle was under way. The members of the gang frequented the houses where the edge-marked cards were used. They played regular games with them and, after their game, they would suggest cutting the pack for high and low.

Large sums of money were staked on this sport. The cards were laid on the table and spread slightly. The secret signals began to peep. The gambler who knew the game could pick any card he wanted any time without a moment's hesitation.

These fellows lost no time in their clean-up. They cut for big stakes, won their money, and got out. The game was pulled simultaneously in many gambling houses and it was done so strongly that people began to suspect.

That was the signal to quit. The gamblers slipped out of the picture, leaving their cards behind them. The packs were examined, but the marks were not discovered. The face of the ace of spades, however, caused considerable comment, for its peculiar skull, crossbones and scimitar formed the insignia of an European secret organization which was notorious all over the continent.

Victims Keep Quiet

When the immensity of the swindle was realized there was nothing to be done about it. The sinister message of the ace of spades made the gambling houses keep quiet, for they were not anxious to incite the wrath of a powerful organization which could do them harm.

Whether the organization was in back of the scheme or not was never learned. No one was anxious to find out. It is possible that the whole thing was framed by a group of gamblers who adopted the ace of spades pattern to protect themselves, knowing that it would shield them.

At the same time it is quite likely that the organization itself was in back of the game and used this method to increase its finances. At any rate, large sums of money changed hands and many persons lost thousands of dollars.

Edge Readers Appear in America

Some time later the same pack appeared in New York and figured in a card-cutting contest where several persons were victimized and lost large sums of money.

By that time the packs were off the market and could not be obtained anywhere. These edge readers were probably the most remarkable pack of marked cards ever made, and when they were designed it seemed impossible that they could be used for any purpose other than that for which they were intended—entertainment.

But the idea was so clever that the gambler on the lookout for something new soon saw a use for it. It is impossible to find the marks on these cards by riffling them unless a person knows to look

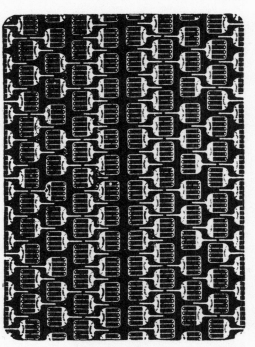

This is the back of the ace of spades. The marks that appear upon it are so tiny and obscure that they are almost invisible when the card is seen alone. But in the pack the card stands out plainly.

along the edge and even then no one can read an individual card. The design of the ace of spades is illustrated here; also the back of the same card, showing how difficult it is to find the mark when the card is there alone!

But the large illustration shows the whole system—so clearly that words are unnecessary to describe it!

Despite the smallness of the marks on a pack of this type, the system is so perfect that close scrutiny is not necessary.

How Gamblers Win at Poker

Sleights and Tricks of the Sharpers—How They Work Together and Evade Detection

The man on the right wants to see if the flush is a real one.

THE picture shows Mr. A. Sapp (center), playing cards with Mr. Sharp and Mr. Sharper, who are swindling him out of his hard-earned cash by teamwork and co-operation.

When a victim with money falls into the clutches of two unscrupulous gamesters he is sure to lose his bankroll and he is generally separated from it under conditions of good-fellowship during a friendly game with high stakes.

Two crooked gamblers can wreak havoc in a game with one, two, or three players against them, for they know how to perpetrate many clever swindles that cannot be detected.

The first game, illustrated above, is called "Spreading the Cards," and it is done very artfully in the course of the evening's play.

First of all the gamblers have a system of signals—simple and natural signs that enable them to tell each other what they hold in their hands. In a friendly game they can often put over many bits of deception, and this is one of the most effective:

The gambler on the reader's left has held a four flush or a three flush (four or three cards of the same suit). He has called for one or two cards on the draw, but he has not filled the flush. Instead he holds just four cards of one suit.

He immediately signals to his confederate that he needs another diamond. The confederate (on the right) has the needed card and signals back O. K.

Note the small explanatory drawings which show what takes place. The man with the four flush palms the undesired card with the back toward the palm of his hand. The other gambler palms the diamond with the face of the card toward his hand. Then

The player with the four-flush palms off the extra card. Then he throws down the four diamonds leaving them squared together.

he drops out of the game and tosses his four remaining cards into the discard, where no one realizes that only four cards have been dropped.

The sharp with the four flush bets his hand to the limit and then throws it on the table when the showdown comes. He says:

"There is a flush. That wins!"

In throwing the alleged flush on the table he does not spread it but leaves the cards clustered together. The sap has only three of a kind, which loses to a flush.

The moment that the fake flush hits the table the sharper on the right says:

"Let's see all the cards—spread them out!"

Suiting the word with the action he extends his right hand with the palmed diamond and spreads the four flush along the table to display the cards. In doing this he drops the palmed card, which makes the fifth diamond needed in the flush. Sure enough, there is the flush and the man on the left takes the pot.

In the meantime he deposits his extra palmed card on top of the pack.

This same system is used to fill

a full house or four of a kind. The sharpers work it back and forth whenever necessary, but they do not employ it too often during one game.

This swindle is a favorite with gamblers who travel on steamships between Europe and America. They appear to be good fellows and get into plenty of card games, where they pay their passage money and expenses and also

put money aside for future use.

Other stunts are used by these players. Suppose one man is dealing and knows what the other has. The dealer waits for the draw and in picking up the deck palms a couple of good cards from his own hand and drops them on the pack when he picks it up. Then in dealing to his companion, who is on the left, he gives his confederate the cards needed in a most natural and offhand manner.

By their simple system of signals these sharps can tell if they cannot aid each other. For example, one man holds two aces. The other has no aces. That makes a bigger possibility of the other aces being in the pack, so the man with two aces draws and tries to fill. In brief, they are playing two hands co-operatively, and that course is sure to win in the long run as it gives a real advantage over the other players.

If the game is supposedly a friendly one, the sharp with the lowest hand will drop out, and as he is no longer in will act indifferently. He knows what his pal is holding and he often manages to glimpse the hand held by the sucker. Immediately he signals his partner to stay in or drop out.

These are the methods which enable gamblers to win.

The confederate adds the extra diamond to the four-flush when he reaches forward to spread the cards across the table.

A needed card is easily gained with the aid of the "hold-out" which operates within the gambler's sleeve.

Card Sharps Exposed

*How Gamblers Win Without Confederates—
Explaining "Hold-outs," "Shiners"
and other Tricks of the Trade*

IN Pullman cars travelers read signs that warn them against playing cards with strangers. This is because there are plenty of bunco men who earn an easy living by riding back and forth on limited trains, looking for suckers who will play for big stakes.

These knights of the pasteboards generally play what is known as the lone hand; that is, they work by themselves and use no confederates. Two gamblers can do much together; but there are times when one man must operate for himself.

The "Hold-out"

The most dangerous device employed by the single-handed gambler is called the "hold-out." The first contrivance of this sort was invented forty or fifty years ago by a man named Kepplinger. He used it when he played with other gamesters—in games where the sky was the limit and everyone was looking for crooked work. His little playmates knew that he was cheating; but they couldn't catch him in the act. So one night they got together and jumped on him. They removed

his coat and found the "hold-out."

The large picture shows how this device is operated. It is a slender, jointed bar, running up the sleeve, as shown in the explanatory diagram. A cord runs to the gambler's trousers and is drawn from one knee to the other. The mere action of separating the knees or pushing them together causes this mechanism to emerge from the sleeve and to go back again. A mechanical clip on the end will steal a card from the gambler's hand or enable him to introduce another card into the game. In brief, the machine steals, adds, or exchanges cards.

The men who found the machine on Kepplinger were well repaid for their discovery. They promised to keep his secret, and in return they were supplied with similar devices. It was not long before other gamblers obtained the information, and "hold-outs" were improved and varied, so that now there are about eight varieties which are manufactured and sold at prices ranging from $25 to $125.

Some of them work through a movement of the arm; others by an expansion of the chest; but each one operates smoothly. One device steals cards through the front of the vest, intead of the sleeve.

Using the "Hold-out"

A player who uses one of these machines can turn the tide of the game whenever he chooses. The "hold-out" carries away an ace every time the player holds one. When he has two or three aces up his sleeve and draws another, he exchanges the hidden aces for two indifferent cards and then lays down the winning hand.

A story has been told of a master gambler who used one of these machines and entered a game with some small-fry gamesters who won their big money with a "cold deck" —as explained elsewhere in this book. The gambler with the machine kept on stowing cards away until he had a Royal Flush up his sleeve.

When the "cold deck" entered the game and he received a high Full House on the deal, he let the "hold-out" do its stuff. It exchanged hands, and he sat pretty with the Royal Flush. When it came to the show-down he had the big winning hand and the other gamblers had been beaten at their own game.

Only the most skilful crooked gamblers use the "hold-out," for it is expensive, and if it is suspected, it may be found in the possession of the gambler, proving him to be crooked.

The Little "Shiner"

Take a game like Red Dog or Black Jack. It all depends upon the card the dealer is about to turn over. If he knows that card, he has a big advantage. Now the gambler playing without a marked pack has no natural method of tell-

ing the card he is about to turn up. With the "shiner" he can do this in a jiffy.

The "shiner" is a small mirror, sometimes concave, like the mirrors used by dentists. Hold one of these under the index corner of a card and the reflection tells the card.

Four types of "shiners" are exposed here.

First is the Ring Shiner. It is sometimes attached to a ring; but the improved type fits in a cameo ring, under the stone, which opens on a hinge. The dealer wears one of these rings. He pushes a card slightly off the top the pack, and when he glances downward he gets a view of the index corner, reflected in the mirror which is turned to the inside of his hand.

He can snap the ring shut in an instant, and thus hide all evidence of the "shiner."

The Pipe Shiner is another form of the mirror gag. No one suspects a pipe that is placed on the table by a player. But this innocent article contains a mirror in the bowl, and the player sets it in a handy position, where he can see the cards as he deals. The mirror is removable, so the player can dispose of it under pretense of knocking ashes from his pipe.

Probably the most ingenious of all "shiners" is the Chip Shiner shown here. The card sharp carries a dummy stack of chips in his pocket. The stack is cut open at one side and a mirror is inserted. As soon as the player has many chips on the table before him he rings in the dummy stack and piles loose chips on top of it. It looks perfectly natural, and the player keeps it surrounded with loose piles of chips, until he is ready to use the "shiner." Then he slides one of the loose piles out of the way, and when he deals the cards he holds them directly above the little mirror. Any time he wants to hide the mirror he pushes the fake stack in among the genuine chips.

The Table Shiner is attached beneath the table, either by a pin or a little suction cup. It can be disposed of quickly and can be turned around so that it is out of sight. While not so ingenious as some of the other contrivances, it is often safer, for it is below the table.

Besides this there are Match Box Shiners—little mirrors set in the end of a box of matches—Tooth Pick Shiners, which are very tiny mirrors for a quill tooth-pick. Some players simply spill a drop of water on a polished table and find that it is effective as a "shiner."

These mirrors are sometimes flat, sometimes concave (hollowed) so that they enlarge the reflection; but others are convex (bulging), so that they reveal the surface of more than just the index corner of a card. This enables the player to catch a glimpse very quickly.

Needless to say, a sharper who can deal from the bottom has a decided advantage when he uses a "shiner." Even marked cards will not disclose the bottom card; but the little mirror tells the tale, and the gambler can use the bottom card whenever he sees fit. If he locates a desirable card on top of the pack, he employs the second deal, dealing the second cards and keeping the top card in place until he is ready to use it.

Crooked Gambling Houses

Card sharps who play the lone game are found under all conditions and in all places. They use one or more of the devices illustrated here, and besides that they have other contrivances equally ingenious.

These men can often obtain work in gambling houses, because they know the ropes and have sense enough not to talk. The man who can quietly stack the cards is always in demand. Many gambling houses use dealers who are quiet-mannered individuals, yet who can deal dynamite.

Lots of men frequent gambling houses and lose plenty of cash, yet think the game is on the level. The house collects a certain percentage of the money put in play. In many

instances this is purely a bluff. The unsophisticated players think that it proves the house is square, because it is getting its percentage, which may amount to quite a lot in one day.

But don't forget that the man who operates a gambling joint must make hay while the sun shines. He is either liable to arrest, or is paying for the privilege of keeping open. If he would be satisfied with a small but regular percentage, he would close up his hang-out and go into a more quiet form of enterprise.

In some of these places the player comes to the door, gives the high sign and is conducted upstairs in what appears to be a quiet club; in fact, it may be a defunct club which still possesses a charter. On the third floor the chips are clinking and the games are in progress. It doesn't cost much to get in, and a conservative player can gamble all afternoon until a bell sounds, when the gang goes up to the fourth floor and a free dinner is served. Then back to the gaming room and away again.

The house makes small profits on drinks, tobacco, etc., but to pay for dealers, attendants, free dinners, and rental of the premises is a big job. The chances are ten to one that the dealers are smooth crooks who employ every means in their power to make certain players win —players who are confederates and who are hired by the house. In their own building the crooks are safe even if they are detected; but they are careful. Otherwise they would drive the suckers away.

Small-time Crooks

The players who sit in the game and get the good hands are lesser gamesters who are clumsy dealers. They have more to do than just sit around and rake in the dough. One of their jobs is to steal as many chips as they can. They do this with a contrivance called the "check-cop." It is a small disc which the player holds concealed in his hand; in fact, it may be

The "check-cop" enables the small-time gambler to steal chips from the pot.

attached to a finger ring. It is smeared with wax, and every time the crook gets his fingers in the chips on the table he presses the "check-cop" against a big chip and takes it away in his hand. In this manner the petty thieves are constantly depriving unsuspecting players of their winnings.

The "check-cop" is used outside of gambling halls by players in friendly games. It is shown on this page, and the picture explains its operation.

The small-time gambler keeps the "check-cop" active in a game where the stakes are high, and he doesn't have to worry much about the cards. He gets his percentage out of every pot, and he won't lose much even if the odds are against him.

The player who is using an ordinary deck can learn methods of false-shuffling, stacking the cards, and executing crooked deals. These are not explained here because they are generally worked with a confederate who cuts the deck at the right place; furthermore, they require complicated maneuvers, and they are a form of information which cannot help the reader. Gamblers can deal off the bottom of the pack or they can deal the second card with ease. Yet the person who knows the method cannot detect the smooth dealer. To explain these tricky movements in detail would help no one in catching a gambler, and this book's purpose is to expose—not to teach.

Loaded tops make "Put and Take" a big game for the crooked gamester.

Put and Take
Methods of Using Crooked Tops

EVERYONE is familiar with the old game of "Put and Take." The apparatus used is a little top, which each player spins in turn. On the sides of the top are markings that say: "Put 1—Put 2—All Put," etc. Also marks that read: "Take 1—Take 2—All Take," etc.

The players put money into the "kitty." Then each one spins the top. Suppose they are playing with dimes. If a player spins "Put 2," he puts two dimes into the "kitty." A spin of "All Put" means that every player contributes a dime.

Sometimes the "kitty" gets very large. Then a player spins "Take All," and he gets the entire "kitty."

Many people have played this game with the regulation tops, which can be bought very cheaply. But many gamblers pay more money and buy crooked tops, which they carry in their pockets and put into a game when they want to make money.

A crooked "Put and Take" top is fixed so that a tap one way will make little weights enter the "Takes," while another tap will put the weights into the "Puts."

Thus the gambler can win whenever he wants to and can make the other players feed the "kitty" as often as he chooses.

This top is illustrated in the explanatory drawings.

Another style of top is also explained. This is an improvement and it will stand rigid examination.

The angles are irregular. That is, the top is slightly out of shape, a fact that is never noticed.

When the top is spun naturally—to the right—these angles cause the "Puts" to come up much more frequently than the "Takes," because the sharp corners tend to stop the roll of the top, while the other angles let it roll by.

As it is a poor rule that does not work both ways, the operator simply spins the top in the reverse direction. This favors the "Takes," just as the ordinary spin favors the "Puts." The result is that the operator is the big consistent winner and the longer the game progresses the better off he is.

A left-hand spinner will unconsciously profit by a top of this nature, for he naturally whirls it in reverse. But the operator does not worry so long as there are plenty of people in the game.

If you play "Put and Take" look out for these crooked tops.

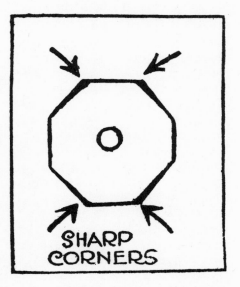

Sharp edges cause the top to favor "puts," except when the crooked player spins.

Open Season on Chumps

THE grifter is back and he's gunning for chumps. So you'd better zip up those pockets, pal.

Again the percentage wheels are spinning, the electric flashers are blinking their lure across the carnival lot, baseballs are popping in and out of buckets, and a new crop of suckers is being measured for the cleaners.

Over all comes the strident voice of the grifter—concessionaire to you—inviting people to "win a big prize for a dime" as the shills step aside politely to let the customers move in where they can close around them. For this has been a lush year for the boys in the skin stores, those who have been lucky enough to stock their joints with flash merchandise that nobody can win. And this season presages even bigger years ahead.

Carnivals of today, if we are to believe the flamboyant claims of their press representatives, have reached the status of a highly respectable entourage, a boon to any community. They are traveling amusement parks, expositions—even Chautauquas, for the benefit of those who have forgotten what a Chautauqua really was. They like to use such names as "Cavalcade" and "Gayway." In actuality these "Magnificently Equipped and Favorably Known Midways" do bring their "Multitudes of New Attractions" since they travel in railroad trains of as many as thirty cars.

Yet with those multitudes, the carnivals still carry concession operators whose business is not to amuse the patrons, but to trim them. For without them, the carnival lot would be barren indeed of prosperous customers, the money spenders who love a chance to take a chance.

To the credit of the carnivals

it must be noted that year by year, permanent amusement parks have been yielding more and more to the persuasion of the concessionaire or grifter, letting him settle right in the local bailiwick. And during the war years, when carnival routes were necessarily curtailed by lack of transportation, this practice increased further. So the carnival and the amusement park have acquired a mutual weakness, but with a certain difference, found in the games themselves.

Long ago, carnival games fell into two classes: games of chance and games of science and skill. Of the two, the first evil was the lesser; so naturally it begat the greater, as all evils do. The mere term "games of chance" so roused public indignation that they were banned in certain communities. Since operators had to operate, they concocted something better. They aptly called it "science and skill," because both were required in the operation of such games. This in turn demanded a bigger "take" as a reward for the operator's ingenuity and trouble.

As of today, the games of chance have gravitated to the amusement parks, while those of "science and skill" ride with the carnivals, although the techniques of trim are interchangeable, whenever occasion or opportunity demands.

The most popular games of chance are "percentage wheels," as they are known in the trade. They stem from the type that became known as the "blanket wheel" because blankets were the principal prize. These were simply big vertical wheels divided into many tiny sections, all numbered. Pins marked the limits of the sections, so that a flexible pointer would be sure to stop in

one division after the wheel ended its spin.

These wheels showed too many numbers, and therefore tended to scare off trade. There were fewer numbers, therefore, on the improved wheels. One popular wheel is numbered only from one to eight, with a chance of winning a dollar—where cash is the stake—on any one of those numbers. This looks wonderful, but, of course, there is a catch. Actually, the wheel has forty divisions, five smaller ones to each of the numbered spaces. Only the central subdivision pays a dollar; the other pairs pay fifty and thirty cents respectively.

It looks like an eight to ten bet. In practice, by the law of averages, the operator takes in four dollars and pays out two dollars and sixty cents.

Top-notcher of the percentage games this year is the "Big Six Wheel," which evades the question of averages by banishing numbers from its resplendent rim that measures fifty-four inches in diameter. The "Big Six" has forty-eight spaces in all, but lacking numbers they are difficult to count, as the wheel is kept too busy to be seldom still. Six of those divisions, at equal distances apart, are adorned with large stars. The other sections run alternately red and black.

The player gets even money on either the red or black; if it plays a star, the terms are five to one. Result: If the "Big Six" operates on a dollar play, the owner takes forty-eight and pays out forty-two, where the colors are concerned, because the stars are neutral. If the players prefer to try the stars, the wheel brings the operator six dollars for every five he returns.

A nice, steady profit this; but

The operator of a crooked percentage wheel says he'll pay you 10 to 1 if the wheel stops at a number corresponding to the number on which you place your money. To make a clean-up he deftly pushes a leaded thumb-tack into the back of the wheel opposite a number that is not being played. How he takes advantage of the law of gravity to take your money is shown in the side-view diagram

it doesn't live up to the vast odds that the wheel men are supposed to make. At least it doesn't until we divulge a by no means closely-guarded secret; namely, that the "Big Six" has a gaff.

And what is a gaff?

In the case of the "Big Six," the gaff is a control rod that runs up through the bulky, ornamental standard to which the wheel is fitted. The rod is operated by a foot pedal underneath the counter, forcing the rod against the axle of the wheel. As one manufacturer of a "Big Six" expresses it, you can "brake it just like your car." Of course the best time to do this is when most of the customers are betting on the stars. Those stars are easily spotted when the turning wheel begins to slacken, and there is plenty of spread between them in which to stop the wheel.

There are simpler ways of gaffing a percentage wheel. A weight built into the framework, or a series of such weights will cause high numbers to ride past the stopping point. Any number on an ordinary blanket wheel can be fixed on an instant's notice by the expedient of pressing a glass-headed push-pin into the back of the wooden rim, the head of the push-pin being

weighted with a short coil of soldering wire. It is inserted near the number on which the big bets have been placed. This brings that number toward the bottom, since the indicator which marks the winning number always projects down from the post above the wheel.

As for putting the percentages far more in the operator's favor than they appear to be, the owner has only to bend some of the projecting nails a trifle downward with a pair of pliers. This is specially applicable to wheels that have certain high-pay brackets, like the eight-number wheel with the dollar sections. The flexible indicator flips over the bent pin when the wheel is stopping there, and winds up in the next—and cheaper—section.

Flashers are a modern development of the old percentage wheel. When electricity began to be wired into the carnival lot, bulbs were attached to the rims of the wheels to give them flash when they revolved. The next development was to have flashing lights themselves denote the winning number, eliminating the wheel entirely.

This is done by spinning a small revolving arm or contact lever, which covers a circle of

plugs or contact posts, set horizontally. The posts are wired to the separate lights on the flasher. Those lights blink rapidly, haphazardly, then slacken and stop on a single light to indicate the winner. Though usually operated on a strict percentage basis, flashers are easily gaffed by slightly depressing certain contact posts. There is still sufficient contact to flicker the bulbs that those posts represent, but the revolving arm slides over such posts as it stops. Thus if blue bulbs are advertised as tokens of bigger prizes, the operator can see to it that the flasher never stops on blue.

Spindles are the counter equivalent of the percentage wheel. They are big arrows with flexible extension pointers, and are set horizontally on the counter. When the operator whirls the arrow, it spins around a circle of upright pins, all separating numbered divisions. Finally the pointer clicks to a stop in what becomes the winning section.

Some spindles have hidden brake-rods that work from behind the counter, but the really cute gaff lies in the upright pins. These are large, substantial and ornamental, of flat metal twisted into spiral shape. Pretty things, these curlicues that rear a few inches from the board, particularly from the operator's viewpoint. For the pins are "set" so that their spiral twists are alternately inward and outward, in relation to the indicator.

By pressing a hidden plunger, the operator lifts the spindle post a fraction of an inch and the gaff can be locked. Thus the pointer slips past every other pin, either odd or even, as the grifter may prefer. The spaces are marked alternately odd and even, or can be painted red and black. In either case, the operator simply sets the gaff against the greater number of players or the larger amount of bets.

A great advantage of a spindle

is that a grifter can often set one up after the local constabulary have "sloughed" the wheels. Slough, pronounced like plough, means to declare a game illegal, forcibly or gently. Spindles are less conspicuous than wheels. Certain varieties, particularly the famous camel-back, can be packed away on an instant's notice. What is more, the camel-back spindle is a most wonderful two-way job, meaning that it can be operated fairly or otherwise.

The improved camel-back consists of two parts: a metal tripod weighing less than two pounds, and a bulky hump-centered arrow that weighs as much as ten. Thanks to a center pivot, the spindle can be placed neatly in the tripod's socket, where it balances perfectly. When the operator gives the spindle an easy twirl, it revolves for a long while because of the relation of its weight to the slight friction that eventaully stops it.

The tripod legs have lugs that fit into counter holes, but this spindle can be operated on any table, even on a sheriff's desk, if he has seized one as an exhibit. But there are no special parts, nothing to prove that the device is crooked, should the owner be hauled into the sheriff's office with it. Yet the grifter could trim the sheriff then and there; provided the sheriff's desk is as creaky as the counter of the carnival booth, as sheriff's desks are apt to be.

Mere hand pressure on the edge of the counter or desk causes the light tripod to tilt at an imperceptible angle and increase the friction of the pivot of the heavier spindle. The slow revolution on the ponderous spindle allows almost perfect control as the grifter leans forward curiously to see where the arrow is about to stop. So responsive is the spindle that it has been called a "creeper"—and its action justifies its title.

Now to probe into the deeper realm of science and skill, though it must be conceded that percentage games have their share of those factors.

In towns where the wheels have been sloughed, or more commonly in communities where they are not tolerated at all, the carnival midway abounds with a surprising variety of intriguing games that offer simple and sometimes curious types of customer participation.

The operator of such a concession, or "joint" as it is termed, is the lineal descendant of a species originally termed a "fakir" and now styled a "grifter." His customers, once called "dupes" later became "suckers," and today are generally classed as "chumps." In swindling or "clipping" these chumps, the grifter is aided and abetted by confederates once known as "cappers," later as "shillabers" or "shills," and in more recent parlance, "sticks."

The grifter has a very considerable investment in his joint. The game itself may cost from thirty-five to two hundred dollars, or more, consisting of the portable booth, the counter, and the "laydown"—the painted oilcloth on which the chumps place their bets. Finally, there is the merchandise, which is often the costliest of all, depending upon how much the concession operator wants to invest to give his joint the proper class.

The merchandise consists of "flash," the big, expensive-looking prizes which only the shills are supposed to win; and "slum," or cheaper stuff, which is delivered to the suckers in varying quantities. Care should be taken in the grifter's choice of slum. One operator once handed out a lot of nail-puzzles, only to have them thrown back at him from the crowd along the midway. After that he switched to paper flags and wedding rings at sixty-five and ninety cents a gross, respectively.

Painted on the joint is the legend "Science and Skill," and the grifter, in his spiel, keeps proclaiming that his concession is "not a game of chance." In buying his game, the grifter has studied the catalogue description very carefully to make sure it contains the statement: "Can be worked strong"—which means the game is "gaffed."

Nobody has yet seen a gaffed game that was not "worked strong," though there are times when the grifter does not need to bother.

Toss or pitching games are a very popular type. The dean among these is the Knife Rack, which consists of a group of shelves, set like steps, studded with open knives fixed point down. Predominant among these are deer-foot hunting knives and, as an added inducement, carving irons are set in sockets along the front shelf, each iron having a valuable prize or a five-dollar bill attached to it by a ribbon.

The player pays a dime for the privilege of tossing a dozen wooden curtain rings at these exhibits. Should he encircle a knife, he wins it; the same applies to the carving-iron prizes. Forty rings for a quarter, a hundred for a dollar, are wholesale bargain offers. The grifter demonstrates that the rings will go over the knife handles; indeed may toss a few on the carving-irons from close range.

But the sucker never wins.

The answer is quite simple. The irons have knobby handles that tilt in one direction; the same applies to the deerfoot handles of the choice hunting-knives. A ring will slide over from one direction, but not the other. The operator simply keeps the narrow ends turned away from the customer. Of course the grifter can slip the rings on the knives from behind; and can twist the carving-irons half around, when demonstrating a short toss of his own, only to reverse the iron again, when removing the ring.

While a customer was playing one of these joints, a friend who was with the grifter and their conversation was only occasionally interrupted by the sucker interposing a dollar bill for another batch of rings. Finally the chump turned empty-handed and said to his friend: "Let's go. I'm broke."

The grifter looked at his new acquaintance, gestured at the chump, and asked in surprise: "Is *he* with *you?*"

Getting a nod in reply, the grifter reached beneath the counter, brought out a huge basket filled with rings and planted it in front of the disappointed player.

"Go ahead and pitch," said the grifter. "I want to talk some more with this friend of yours."

The sucker still didn't win a knife—not by a free basketful.

Hoop-La is another deceptive tossing game.

Here the player tries to toss hoops over square blocks covered with velvet, each block being topped with a clock, a cigarette case, or some other attractive prize. To win, the hoop must gird the entire block, and lie flat on the platform. The hoops are the light wooden type used for embroidery work. As a result they always bounce and invariably land titled over one corner of the block; though the operator can carefully drop one around the block, just to prove that a win is possible.

A gaff is ordinarily unnecessary with a Hoop-La block, but one is available if the grifter wants to display some really valuable prize, such as a genuine gold watch of warranted make. The gaffed block is made in three-ply wood, so that the center layer can be pressed out of alignment through the velvet. This hidden device makes it impossible for the hoop to gird the

block, but the operator can demonstrate otherwise, simply by pressing the center segment back to normal.

Pitching pennies has always been a popular sport, so concession operators were quick to adopt an item called the Penny Board, where coins tossed on a slanted board set off an electric bell when they contact small brass discs. The board measures thirty by forty-five inches, so its forty discs are quite trivial in relation to the area. Statistics show an average of twenty-six tosses for each win, and the usual prize is an eight-cent box of candy, a more-than-comfortable profit.

From this, however, developed a still more profitable pitch game, which costs the operator nothing to manufacture, since he uses the prizes as the target. In a roped-off square are packages of cigarettes, with a sprinkling of Lucky Strikes among them. The Luckies are the target; if you can toss a penny so it lands inside the circles trade-mark, you win any pack of cigarettes on display.

This is literally a self-gaffed game. The gaff is the cellophane. Pennies just won't stay on it. They slide off continually, and when he closes his joint for the night the grifter sweeps them up, after putting away the cigarettes. He must remember, though, to use fresh cigarettes packs after several days, as the cellophane loses its slick from the friction of the passing pennies.

Similarly, the ducks have to be changed quite often in the good old game of Duck Pond. These are live ducks that go as prizes to anyone who can toss a hoop around one's neck. Nobody wins, because nobody can toss a hoop more cleverly than a duck can dodge it; but eventually the ducks become accustomed to the flying hoops and make no effort to avoid them. Then the grifter has to swap his veteran ducks for

a flock of hoop-shy recruits.

Duck Ponds have been barred in many localities by anti-cruelty societies. These same groups stopped the use of canaries as carnival prizes after discovering that grifters were spending their spare time catching sparrows and dipping them in gilt paint. This is but typical of the grifter's perpetual effort to please his public—at least long enough until he clears town. Concessionaires are always searching for cheap substitutes for slash, so they can throw some sizeable-appearing prizes at the customers, rather than use shills as business boosters.

For shills are a heavy operating item with such concessions as the Pop-in Buckets, which rate as a cross between a tossing and a throwing game. The grifter keeps offering baseballs while proclaiming "Pop 'em in the bucket! Pop 'em in the bucket! Three balls for a dime!" And ready customers step up to prove that they can do it.

The bucket is set in an open framework, slanted toward the customers. Surrounding the bucket is a net, and there is a hole in the front of the bucket, near the bottom. The game is to toss a baseball into the bucket and have it roll out through the little hole. This looks easy, as the toss is short and the wooden bucket quite wide.

It *is* easy, for the first customers—who are shills. But by the time they are walking away with prizes, other players, the chumps, are finding that the game requires more skill than they supposed. Their baseballs hit the bottom of the bucket and bounce out, so they start tossing them harder, straighter; or attempt to give them a tricky spin.

The suckers are licked before they begin. By merely changing the tone of his blatant "Pop 'em in the bucket!" the grifter has called for the gaff, which is supplied by a hidden helper. This assistant pulls a cord, operating a plunger in the false bottom of the bucket. This presses a disk up against the inner bottom, making the latter firm, so the balls will bounce out. When the plunger is released for the benefit of the shills, the bucket bottom goes dead and the balls no longer bounce.

As one grifter puts it: "We ought to call these Pop-*out* Buckets instead of Pop-ins, except that the chumps would get wise—or would they?"

Probably they wouldn't. For this season's most popular throwing game is Big Tom, one of the simplest and oldest flim-flams in the trade, but the chumps of the Atomic Age are falling for it heavier than ever. Big Tom is the name of a stuffed canvas cat who squats thirty inches high and sits on a portable stand behind a low, ornamental sign which either bears his name or the statement "Knock Me Off." So the patrons wham away with baseballs and keep knocking Big Tom down, but not off his rack.

Since a knock off is necessary to gain a prize, no prizes are given out—except to shills. The sticks invariably topple Big Tom from his perch. The base of the stuffed cat is heavily weighted, and the sign fixed in front of the figure is a solid portion of the stand. Because of the bottom weight, the cat can only be knocked flat, not off the stand, because the sign prevents hits from striking low enough to jounce the figure backward. When the customers throw, the operator sets Big Tom close to the front; but when he wants a shill to demonstrate how easy it is, he places the stuffed cat several inches further back. This brings the center of gravity past the rear edge of the stand, when the cat is toppled and Big Tom tumbles.

Despite the revival of the Cat Rack, the Milk Bottle Stand is still the leader in the field of throwing games. Six imitation milk bottles are stacked in pyramid form and three throws are allowed to knock the entire lot from their stand, with special prizes if the job is done in fewer throws. The "bottles" are made of aluminum, which makes a nice crashing sound when they fall. Sometimes the whole stock will scatter from one swift, well-aimed pitch.

Of course, that's when a shill is pitching. The sucker can't succeed, even with three fine throws. Though the bottles look alike, three are heavies, the other three lightweights. Put the heavies on top and a low throw will knock the props from under them. That's the set-up when the shill throws; for the sucker, it's just the reverse. The three heavies form the bottom row, hence they merely topple and refuse to roll beyond the raised rim of the stand.

Sometimes the operator tops the pyramid with a heavy bottle, but places the other two on the bottom row. Then the chump knocks off four instead of only three. This makes him think he's getting better, and he keeps on throwing. For those who are interested in specifications and prices, the light bottles weigh twenty ounces each and cost two dollars apiece; the heavies scale at three pounds and are priced at three dollars. The extra weight is provided by steel balls which are permanently sealed in a well, or false bottom, of an otherwise hollow bottle.

The light and heavy principle applies to a game so different from the milk bottles that even grifters have been fooled by it. This is a game called English Pool, which consists simply of a felt-covered alley, twenty inches wide by fifty-two in length, with a full-width pocket at the far end. Down near that end is a circle in which rests a pool ball.

The operator puts a coin on the circle ball, then gives the customer another ball and a cue, inviting him to knock the remote ball from its circle and send the coin out with it. A few trials prove that this can be done, and from then on the game is played for keeps, which means that the operator keeps all the money bet. Whether the player shoots the cue ball slow or fast, with a draw or a follow, he can't send the coin from the circle. It always drops within the ring when the supporting ball is shot from under it.

This game has a clue—both balls are white.

Even that clue is slender until from it we deduce that *either* ball could be placed within the circle. Since the balls are identical in appearance, any difference would therefore be in weight. Rudimentary—and true.

Using the lightweight for the cue ball means that the coin will drop when the heavy is knocked from beneath it. But when the heavy serves as cue ball, it packs an added wallop that knocks the coin clear of the circle, along with the light ball. By hefting the balls as he reclaims them from the wide pocket, the operator can plant the light or heavy within the circle, according to how he wants the customer to fare.

This game builds by letting the chump try it for himself, hence shills are luxuries. One day a carnival man who fancied himself a pool shark became intrigued by the game and wanted to try it just for fun. The operator let the carnie knock the coin clear with a very special English shot and from then on gave him the winning cue ball.

So the carnie hung around the joint and whenever business lagged, he showed the suckers how to win, by taking over on their free shots. Of course he gave the operator the wink, to assure him that no chump could master that very nifty English; in fact, none of them succeeded with it, though they played it when they paid.

And at the end of the brisk evening, the carnival man dropped by again and asked: "How about my cut?"

The operator lifted a surprised eyebrow. "For what?"

"For shilling," replied the carnie. "Do you think the monkeys would have kept on biting if they hadn't seen the way my English clicked?"

"Teach me the shot," suggested the operator. "If I can use it, I'll split tonight's take with you."

The volunteer shill never colected. From then on, he was handed the losing cue ball. He's wondering yet how he suddenly lost mastery of that perfect English shot.

There are other games that have mystified the carnival folk themselves. The Swinging Ball did it when first introduced. This game is still a puzzler to greenhorns on the lot, and clips the regular customers season after season. The properties are simple—a bowling ball hanging from a framework above a ten-pin which is set on a peg in the counter.

The grifter demonstrates the game by coming out in front. He takes the bowling ball and gives it a lazy swing past the top of the ten-pin, on the right. The ball returns and knocks the ten-pin over. Setting up the ten-pin, the operator teaches the customer how to do it. After a few trials, the chump succeeds.

From then on, chump is right. When he puts cash on the game, the customer loses the knack. Perhaps he is too eager, too excited. The big, lazy bowling ball always swings too wide to the left on its return. The patient grifter shakes his head and takes the money; then looks for a man with stronger perseverance to play the game—and finds plenty of applicants.

The gaff to this is singularly neat. The hole in the bottom of the ten-pin is just a trifle off center. According to the direction in which the operator turns the ten-pin, the greater portion of its bulk is to the right or left of the peg on which it is set.

The ball is hung so that when the ten-pin is bulking to the left, a swing just barely to the right of the ten-pin will come back and score a hit. If the ten-pin is bulked to the right, the forward swing must necessarily be more to that side and therefore will return wider on the left, missing the ten-pin entirely.

There is something to the claim of "science and skill" where the Swinging Ball is concerned!

In contrast, let us consider that most modern of grindstores, the Blower. The term "grind" refers to a game that keeps on going and going, usually at a nickel a try. Little money but a lot of it. Slum prizes if any. That's the Blower.

The thing intrigues at first sight. Beyond a counter, the patron sees a great square-shaped funnel from which a blast of air is perpetually gushing upward. Surging, gushing amid that current are multitudes of spinning ping-pong balls that are sucked down into the vortex, only to bob up happily again.

The operator, often a smiling girl, thrusts a small net with a long handle into the whirl of celluloid and scoops a ball up and out. She shows you a number on the ball, tosses it back into the mechanized tornado and scoops out another. Every ball has a different number and some of those numbers represent big prizes. The girl scoops out a winner, points to the prize and suggests that it's your turn—for a nickel.

The customer leans across the counter, dips the net into whirling balls and scoops a loser. He scoops and scoops. Always losers. The sweet young grifter scoops and nets a winner. The science is to follow the ball with your eye when she tosses it back in the current, which you can't do amid all that swirl. The skill is to net the winning ball if you do follow it. But you never do that either.

On the grifter's side of the counter, there is a distinct advantage. It is possible to dip down into the bottom of the swirl and cup a ball which is bobbing low amid the ping-pong maelstrom. From across the counter, you can't dip deep enough to do the same. And the winning balls prefer the low altitude. They never bob high enough for the customer to get. Yet they spin normally, in fact perfectly, just like the losers.

The winning ping-pong balls have been inoculated. The method is surprising, yet simple. They are jabbed with a hypodermic containing an injection of mercury. A scientific treatment, skillfully delivered. Science, however, takes first claim.

Skill, on the contrary, leads in the game of Spot the Spot. This is the only pastime of the famous "Three Card Monte" or "Shell Game" family that is still allowed to operate openly on a Midway and as a result it holds a unique appeal.

On an oilcloth laydown are painted three large red spots, each five inches in diameter. The customers who stand before these are provided with five metal disks apiece, each disk measuring slightly more than three inches across. The business is to drop the disks—not place them—so they completely cover the big spot.

Nobody ever wins, so it is best never to try.

Even if the spot were perfect, you'd have trouble covering it completely. But to make it certain that you won't win, the spot is slightly out of shape and can only be covered by dropping the first disk on the bulge. Where

The "red spot game" is found at almost any carnival. All you have to do to win a prize is to drop five metal disks so they will cover a painted circle. But unless you discover a trick bulge in the circle and cover that bulge first, some portion of the circle always will remain exposed. A crooked operator knows where the bulge is by the aid of a very fine mark that a player would not notice

the bulge is, only the operator knows, and in these progressive times the spot is adjustable because the latest models are painted on rubberized oilcloth which can be stretched to suit the individual grifter.

Shills mooch in and out of this game as if they owned it. That's the reason why there are three spots on the laydown, so a pair of sticks flank a customer and give him the squeeze. Thus bracketed, the chump sees people winning on his left and right, for the shills, like the grifter, know where the spots are lopsided. They keep gathering the moola, and the grifter, feigning desperation, keeps boosting the ante to get back his cash.

And the dupe is sucked up, for nature abhors a vacuum, mental as well as physical.

For there is a special trick that makes this almost impossible game look easy. The grifter keeps reiterating that the spot must be completely covered, and that means every speck. Yet even the men who know where and how to drop the spots are lucky to do a perfect job one try

in a dozen. Prolonged scrutiny of the disks will almost invariably show a tiny trace of red peeking somewhere through the overlapping silver.

The grifter never studies a situation long enough to discover if the shills have missed. When a stick covers the spot sufficiently to convince the casual eye, the grifter takes a short glance, announces: "That's it!" and pays off. But when the chump thinks he has won, particularly when the stakes have mounted up to dollars, the grifter holds everything.

Then the sucker's layout is given a microscopic scrutiny. The sticks forget their own play to have a look too, acting as though they hope their fellow-player has won. But when the grifter finally discovers a dot of tell-tale red, the sticks sadly agree that the chump has lost.

Spot the Spot is the Black Widow of the Midway—the smallest but deadliest swindle that ever poisoned a bankroll. The whole layout costs a mere five dollars, disks included; can be carried in the pocket and set up for play on any counter.

In direct contrast stands the High-Striker.

This magnificent contrivance demands an investment of several hundred dollars, requires a

crew to set it up, and runs to a quarter of a ton in shipping weight. It is the colossus of the Fair Grounds, towering higher than anything on the lot, except the Ferris Wheel.

The High-Striker consists of a forty-foot standard marker with numbers up to three thousand, topped by a ten-inch gong. At the bottom is a bumper, or striking beam, and up the standard runs a wire which serves as a track for a small steel weight known as a Chaser.

Customers are furnished with huge wooden mallets, or mauls. They use these to clout the striking beam and drive the chaser up the wire track. Number scores don't count, except for side bets. The real job is to make the chaser hit the gong. Three hits in a row and the customer can have any prize he wants—even the High Striker.

For the victim never rings the bell more than once or twice, if at all.

Brawny shills belt the bumper and gather lesser prizes by occasionally ringing the gong. This encourages the "marks"—a term used to define a specific type of sucker, in this case the local strong boys. But the harder these victims wallop, the less their luck. Some baffling technique seems necessary to ride the chaser clear up to the gong. It wabbles about halfway up, halts, and does an ignominious flop.

For the High-Striker is gaffed, and ingeniously.

The tall standard is braced by long, slanted cables that serve as guy-lines. One cable is actually an extension of the wire track that runs up to the gong. It is purposely left loose; therefore the wire wabbles when the chaser rides it.

But over where the guy-line is fastened to the ground stands a lounger who is studying the banners of a girl show across the Midway. He is the High-

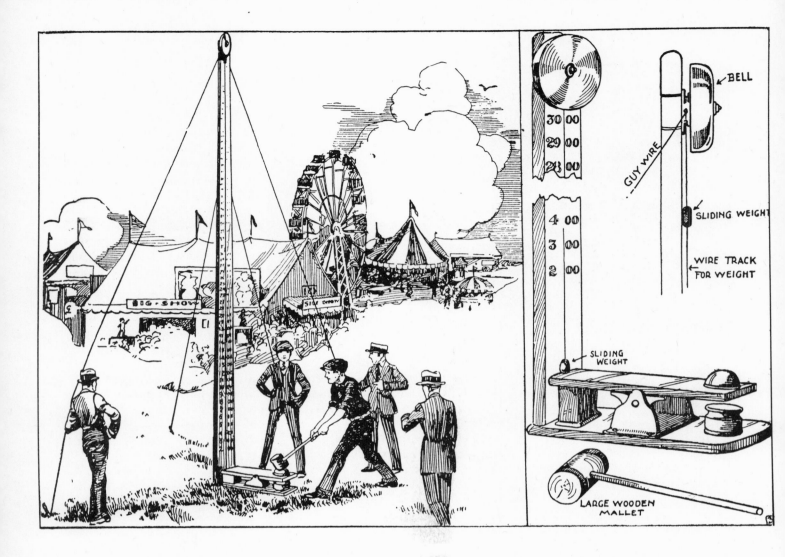

Striker's remote control. When the operator pipes the word, this gentleman leans his shoulder against the guy-line, taking up its slack and that of the wire track. A shill swings the maul and the chaser bangs the gong.

Since the High-Striker often brings dividends in proportion to its size, there are times when the owner can afford to throw a prize, if only as an added come-on. After the husky townies have exhausted themselves without scoring a single gong-hit, the grifter beckons to some gawky youth and talks him into spending a dime, on the basis of a dollar win if he hits the gong just once.

While the big boys smile contemptuously, the grifter pipes the word. The lounger leans as the weakling swings the maul. Up zings the chaser, *clang* goes the gong, and the grifter thrusts a dollar into the hand of the gaping winner, who is staring upward with the rest of the crowd, more amazed than anyone else.

A smart showman, the grifter. Usually his motto is "All for One and All for One," but occasionally he relaxes that rule. For behind his dead-pan dwells a sense of humor which he is willing to indulge at his own expense.

His fun with the High-Striker proves it.

Three-Card Monte

THREE-Card Monte is the grand old game of the bunco man. It is a time-worn swindle that never grows old. Although the large, elaborate fair games have overshadowed it in popular favor, the clever gentleman who throws the cards and invites you to "find the lady" is always hovering in the background, ready to entrap a sucker, and then depart for a new field.

Try the fancy games, if you will: a few dimes or quarters lost may prove an investment, for they will bring practical experience. But when you see a smart young man throwing the three cards then beware! For if you listen to his silvery words, you and your bank roll will soon part company.

All that the "monte man" needs is a table and three playing cards. In a pinch, a soapbox will serve his purpose, or a newspaper opened out and held by two persons is sufficient. Then, aided by his wily confederates, he is ready to prove that Barnum was right.

Let us follow the adventures of Honest John Doe, who visits the fair grounds on a Saturday night, with $50 safely tucked away, where no slick pickpocket can reach it.

John takes a ride in the Ferris wheel, and just as it is about to start a stranger steps in and sits down beside him. For a while, there is silence.

Then, during the third revolution, while they are high above the "midway," the stranger starts a conversation. By the time the ride is finished, they are boon companions. The stranger has given John a drink of "good licker," and has invited him to "walk down the line," and watch a game that is "real sport."

The game is going on behind

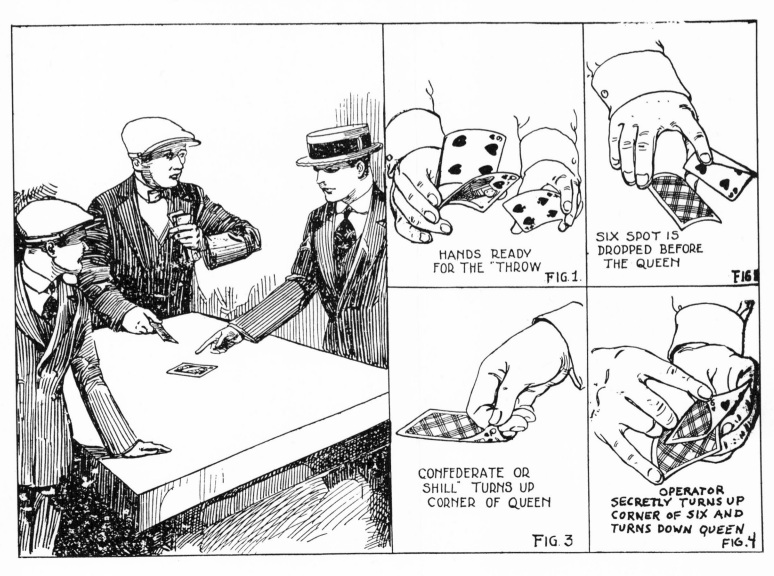

HANDS READY FOR THE "THROW FIG. 1.

SIX SPOT IS DROPPED BEFORE THE QUEEN F16

CONFEDERATE OR "SHILL" TURNS UP CORNER OF QUEEN FIG. 3

OPERATOR SECRETLY TURNS UP CORNER OF SIX AND TURNS DOWN QUEEN FIG. 4

one of the tents. The operator holds three cards, two in his right hand and one in his left. A queen is the bottom card in his right hand (See Fig. 1). He throws the cards; first the queen, then the four, then the six; and one of the players bets a dollar that he can "find the queen." He lays down the money and turns up the card. It is the six of hearts! The player walks away in disgust.

But when Joe arrived on the scene, accompanied by the "shill," a bigger game was automatically instituted. The "shill" bent up the corner of the queen, as shown in Fig. 3. But when the operator put the queen and the six-spot into this right hand he made the deft movement shown in Fig. 4. With his right forefinger he bent up the corner of the six-spot, while his little finger bent down the turned-up corner of the queen. He took the four-spot in his left hand and made a quick throw. Of course, the money was bet on the card with the turned-up corner—and the swindle was accomplished.

"Huh," grunts John. "I'd like to see him fool me." Again the cards are thrown. John throws down a dollar, and turns up a card. It is the queen. The operator pays him a dollar and John smiles with satisfaction. Again he wins; but the third time he

loses. He hands the operator a dollar. It flutters to the ground and the "monte man" stoops to pick it up. With a quick wink, John's companion reaches forward, picks out the queen and bends up its corner as it lies on the table. (See Fig. 3). The operator rises and arranges the cards for another throw. With a quick toss of each hand he drops them on the table. The card with the bent corner stands out plainly.

"Any bets?" questions the operator. John's companion promptly lays a $20 bill on the table. John reaches down into his coat pocket, pulls out two twenties and two fives and deposits them alongside.

"I can't take two bets," says the operator.

"We'll both bet on the same card," replies John's companion. After a moment's hesitation the "monte man" consents.

"Pick out your card," he says. "Find the lady."

John reaches forward, seizes the bent corner of the queen, and triumphantly turns up the card. It is the six of hearts! He stands for a moment in a daze. The operator turns up the next card and shows it to be the queen. He pockets John's fifty, and the stranger's twenty, and is gone. When John has recovered sufficiently, he finds himself alone. His newly found friend

has also departed, chagrined, no doubt, at his stupidity in losing the $20. John starts out to find the sheriff.

But in the meantime a big touring car is speeding away from the fair grounds. At the wheel is the "monte man"; beside him is John's companion; and each one has a $20 bill and a five, securely tucked away in his vest pocket.

John's newly found friend, needless to say, was a "shill"—a confederate of the operator. How he and the "monte man" worked the swindle is shown in the explanatory diagram.

The operator held the cards as shown in Fig. 1. In throwing them he first dropped the queen; then the four of spades, from the left hand; and finally the six of hearts. When the cards were thrown in that manner, any one could follow the course of the queen. If a small sum—two or three dollars—was bet, the operator made the throw as shown in Fig. 2. He shifted the outer end of the queen to his second finger, so that the six-spot was dropped before the queen. This movement can be made so deftly and rapidly that the eye cannot follow it. The player is almost certain to pick the six-spot as the queen.

The Shooting Gallery

THE shooting gallery is seen at nearly every amusement park in the United States. It is the mecca of every boy, for the desire to handle a "real gun," and blaze away at targets, clay pipes, and the like is universal.

Nearly everyone has seen a typical shooting gallery, with its row of "bull's-eyes," the racks populated by clay ducks, the rows of moving targets, the mechanical Indian, who cautiously raises his head from behind an imitation boulder, and the glittering steel balls that dance fan-

tastically on top of streams of water, rising and falling with a suddeness that thwarts the aim of the keenest marksman.

Truly, the shooting gallery is an institution, and it is a form of innocent amusement that will survive as long as parks and fairs retain their popularity.

The proprietor of the up-to-date shooting gallery has a paying proposition if he is situated in a good locality. The charges are usually three shots for a dime, or ten for twenty-five cents. The clay targets are cheap and the metal targets and "bull's-eyes"

last a long time. The great majority of galleries, therefore, are clean-cut. They are conducted "on the square," and the man who seeks diversion receives his money's worth when he patronizes a first-class shooting emporium.

It must be remembered that the proprietor of the gallery has considerable money tied up in his establishment. If he is located in a city he has his regular patrons, and is in the same category as any reputable merchant who seeks a regular list of customers. He gives value for money received and profits accordingly.

But such is not always the case with the "wild cat" galleries—the traveling establishments run by carnival "grifters" who come to the fairs hoping for a quick profit. Such galleries are frequently run on the same basis as the "joints" of the bunco men. That is, the operator is ready at any time to "take in a sucker" and make some easy money.

The procedure, in instances of this sort, is interesting, to say the least. The bunco man is leaning back behind his counter, waiting for business. Along comes a keen-eyed individual, who pays a quarter and fires ten well-directed shots that bring down the moving targets. The customer decides to take ten more shots. He peels off a bill from a roll and pays the operator. The bunco man begins to take interest. He decides to relieve the marksman of some of his wealth before he loses it on the "wheels" and other gambling devices.

"You've got a good eye, brother," he ventures, as an opening statement.

"Yeah," says the stranger, "I've done a good bit of shooting in my time."

The conversation once begun, the operator continues it, reloading the customer's gun, and giving him a free round of shots. The result is that the proprietor and the stranger decide to enter into a friendly shooting competition, with a small bet on the outcome. First one wins, then the other, until finally the bets are raised, and each puts down $10 for a shooting match on the smallest "bull's-eye." This "bull's-eye" is a white metal target, backed by a gong. There is a small hole in the center; so small in fact, that a bullet can just pass through it. The gongs behind the other "bull's-eyes" are all of different sizes, so that the difficult target has a distinctive "ring" that leaves no doubt when hit.

Both men blaze away at the target. When the smoke has cleared away the bunco man leads by two hits, and pockets the twenty dollars. If the player tries to regain his loss in another contest the outcome is the same and he loses $10 more. He finally decides to quit and leaves the premises marveling at the operator's skill and regretting his hastiness in so willingly entering the contest.

The operator, however, is not so clever a marksman as one would suppose. The real cause of his success lies in the strip of black cloth that is stretched across the gallery just above the most difficult target. Behind this cloth, directly above the tiny "bull's-eye," is a hidden gong (see explanatory diagram), the exact duplicate of the one behind the target. The bunco man did not aim at the "bull's eye" at all. He directed his shots at the hidden gong—an easy thing to hit—and so made the winning score.

Sometimes the wary operator will shoot with one hand, or will try trick shots to give his opponent a "handicap." Needless to say, the outcome will still be in his favor.

The Candy Wheel

ANY carnival game which calls for a five-cent "play" is very popular among carnival gamesters. In such a game the player has only five cents at stake and, accordingly, is much more ready to take a chance. He will part with a store of nickels in preference to risking a dime or a quarter on a higher-priced game.

Five-cent games are termed "grindstones" by the bunco men, and the "Candy Wheel" has become their favorite method of swindling the public. Nearly every "midway" at fair or carnival has its candy wheel,

except in localities where the contrivance is branded as a "game of chance," and is not permitted by the authorities.

A typical "Candy Wheel" is shown in the large illustration. The wheel is divided into twenty sections, each section being sub-divided into three parts. Along the counter in front of the wheel is a strip of oilcloth divided into twenty numbered sections, to correspond with the numbers on the wheel. The oilcloth is called a "lay down," because each player lays down a nickel on whichever section he desires to play.

When all twenty sections have been "covered," the operator spins the wheel. After whirling for a short time it finally slows down and stops at one of the numbered sections. It will be seen that the sections are separated by nails which are set near the outer rim of the wheel. A leather indicator is used to designate the winning section, so that there can be no controversy about the wheel stopping on a line.

If the indicator points to the center sub-division of the winning number, the player receives a two-pound box of candy. If it stops at one of the other two subdivisions, the winner receives a one-pound box.

Every time the operator spins the wheel, he takes in one dollar, as there are twenty sections at five cents each. If he loses a two-pound box he puts out only fifty cents, as the box costs him about that sum. Thus he makes a profit of fifty cents on the spin. If he loses a one-pound box, his profit is seventy cents, as the box costs him about thirty cents. Thus, if the law of averages holds good, the operator pays out $1.20 for every $3 he takes in. No wonder the "Candy wheel" is a popular device among the operators, when one considers the profits it yields!

Many operators are content to play the "Candy Wheel" on a strict percentage basis. Even when played "fairly," it is a swindle device, as the profits are so greatly inflated. But the dyed-in-the-wool "bunco man" is not satisfied to let the players win anything if he can help it. Accordingly he attaches a "gaff" or secret contrivance to the wheel. The concealed mechanism is illustrated in the explanatory diagram.

The wheel is mounted on a wooden post, or upright. The axle of the wheel extends through the upright, which is behind the wheel. When the wheel is revolved the axle revolves also. The post, however, is hollow, and contains a metal rod, or plunger, as illustrated. If the plunger is pushed up it presses firmly against the axle, and acts as a brake which stops the wheel.

The plunger connects with a foot lever, which is hidden beneath the counter at the bottom of the poll. When the wheel begins to slow down in its revolution, the operator pushes his foot on the lever, pushing the plunger against the axle. By careful application of the "brake" he is thus enabled to stop the wheel at virtually any number. Among the players is a "capper" or a "shill"—a confederate of the operator. The "shill" places money on one or two of the numbers and the operator causes the wheel to stop at one of the numbers which the confederate has "covered."

Sometimes the operator allows a player to win, but stops the wheel so cleverly that it never comes to rest on one of the two-pound spaces. This, of course, decreases the operator's out-put and adds materially to his profits.

Trick Shuffleboard

IN a previous article the writer emphasized the fact that electrical devices are superseding the old-time games at carnivals and country fairs. Not only do the brilliant lights attract larger crowds than did the antiquated swindle games, but in many localities, electrical games have gained the approval of the authorities; in fact, at many seashore resorts practically all the gambling devices are operated by electricity.

Carnival games are divided into two classes; those which operate on a "percentage," which favors the operator; and those requiring "science and skill,"

where the player apparently holds his fate in his own hands. Hitherto, all electrical games were of the former class; but during the past season, a game appeared which was quite unique—a game of "science and skill" operated by electricity.

Among the gamesters, this new device carries the rather ambiguous title of "The Electric Washer Joint"; its more pretentious name is "Carnival Shuffleboard." The illustration above shows the game ready for operation.

At the end of a sort of alley, or shuffleboard, are twelve bolts, set in the wood, so that their heads barely project. The draw-

ing shows the exact arrangement. The bolts are set in pairs. The player steps up to the front end of the alley, and pays ten cents for the privilege of sliding six washers along towards the set-in bolts. If one washer forms a contact between the two bolts of any pair, one of six incandescent lamps is lighted, and the player is entitled to a small box of candy as a prize; if he succeeds in lighting two, three, four or all six incandescent lamps he receives larger prizes, according to the chart which is displayed at the end of the alley.

It is quite a difficult matter to successfully slide a washer to touch and stay in contact with two adjacent bolt-heads, and the player who wins a prize usually more than earns it. But there is bigger bait held out for the "suckers" who indulge in "Carnival Shuffleboard." It will be observed that the two center incandescent lamps are red. If the player succeeds in making a contact that will light one of these, he receives ten dollars in cash; if he puts on both red lights, he receives twenty dollars; while if he succeeds in lighting all six incandescent lamps, he gains an award of fifty dollars.

This is a remarkable offer, and it is little wonder that the shuffleboard is popular among the players wherever it is introduced. But the most remarkable part is the fact that no one ever wins the cash prizes, and the operator usually "cleans up" a tidy sum from the unsuspecting public.

A close study of the game will convince one that the cash offers could not be *bona fide;* however, any one imbued with the gambling fever is apt to hesitate at nothing. But the man viewing the game from the practical standpoint soon wants to know "where the trick is."

As far as the white lights are concerned, everything is above board. Sometimes the game is played with white lights only, four lamps being used. The prizes are not really so valuable as they appear, and the operator is sure of an enormous profit, without resorting to fraud. But the red lights with their large cash awards are the great attraction; so the wily operator uses

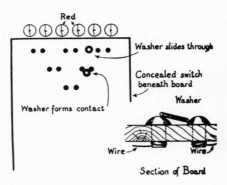

them also, and incorporates a concealed mechanism that enables him to disconnect them without detection.

The explanatory diagram shows the arrangement of wiring beneath the shuffleboard, and reveals the swindle. (A-A), (B-B), etc., represent the pairs of bolts as seen beneath the board, looking up at the bottom.

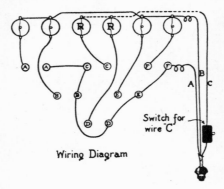

Wiring Diagram

One bolt of each pair is connected to a main wire (A) through which the current passes; the other bolt of each pair leads to one of the incandescents. Two other wires, (B) and (C), are connected with the incandescents; (B) with the white lights; (C) with the red. These wires join wire (A) and run to socket. When the current

is on, the circuit is complete except for the gaps between each pair of bolts. If a washer is laid on bolts (F) and (F), the circuit is completed, and the white light on the right lights up.

Bolts (C-C) and (D-D) supply the contact points for the red lamps. But wire (C), before it joins wires (A) and (B), is controlled by a switch. This switch is conveniently located and hidden underneath the board at one side. The operator, demonstrating the "fairness" of the game, pushes a washer on each pair of bolts (on top of the board), using a glass rod as a pusher. All the incandescents light up. But as he reaches over and slides the washers off the bolts, his other hand, resting on the side of the board, secretly turns off the concealed switch. The red lights are now dead; and so are the player's chances of winning a cash prize!

Of course, at any time, the operator may prove that all the incandescents are active, by merely turning on the switch as he drops a washer onto two adjacent bolts. If some one slides a washer on to bolts (C-C) or (E-E), he will not be surprised if they do not light, for the operator explains that a perfect contact has not been formed.

If only four white lights are employed, the secret switch is not necessary, for the odds are in the operator's favor; but he may offer a grand prize for lighting all four lights; in which case, he will find it advisable to use a controlling switch that will eliminate one of the white lights.

The Flashing Flag

BLUE WINS BLANKET.
RED WINS TOWEL SET.
WHITE WINS BOX of CANDY

TOUCHES BUT SLIDES OVER

WHITE   BLUE   RED   WHITE   BLUE

BLUE PLUG POST SET IN DEEP.

I IS interesting to study how the bunco games and methods of carnival fakers are made more efficient by new inventions, just as legitimate enterprises undergo improvements.

In the "good old days" the "grifter" whirled his wheel of chance in a booth lighted by lanterns. Then came the days of acetylene illumination, and now, when a carnival visits a busy community, a corps of electricians is needed to attach a wiring system to the electric light plant of the town. On Monday night every amusement device, from the Ferris wheel to the smallest

concession, bursts forth in a blaze of glory, and the astonished citizen finds a veritable "gay white way" transported to his doorstep.

Not long after electricity became established as the means of illumination for the "midway" of the fairs and carnivals, an enterprising "grifter" discovered that a series of lights attached to his "percentage wheel" produced a flash that drew an unprecedented number of customers to his booth. Illuminated wheels then became the rage, and were soon seen everywhere.

Then the "flasher" was invented. In its original form it was a

sort of stationary wheel, studded with incandescent lights. Instead of the wheel revolving, the light skipped from bulb to bulb—only one incandescent being lighted at a time. Finally the original idea was elaborated, fancy boards replaced the plain wheel, and now one of the most recent developments has been attained in the "Flashing Flag."

The use of the American flag in advertising devices has been restricted. Why its use in a gambling device is not prohibited is hard to say. The "Flashing Flag" is not a replica of Old Glory, but when it is studded with red, white and blue incandescents, the resemblance is close enough to draw the crowd, as the average visitor to the fair is apt to mistake it for a patriotic display, and the device draws big business on the Fourth of July and other holdiays, when customers are numerous.

On the flag shown in the drawing there are forty-five lights, fifteen red fifteen white and fifteen blue. Each group is numbered from one to fifteen. The red and white lights form alternate stripes, while the blue are in the field.

On the oilcloth "laydown" on the counter are fifteen squares. Fifteen players enter the game, each depositing a dime on his particular square. The operator turns on the current and a metal arm begins to revolve in a small box which is set on the counter. (See upper explanatory diagram.) The end of the metal arm forms a contact with a circle of posts. Just as it passes one it reaches the next in the circle. Each contact controls a different incandescent, so that the light leaps in a haphazard manner from bulb to bulb. Finally the current is turned off. The metal arm continues to revolve, until it comes to a stop, forming a contact with one of the posts. The bulb controlled by that post remains lighted and the man who has his money on a square corresponding in number to the

lighted bulb receives a prize.

The size of the prize depends upon the color of the winning light. White entitles the player to a box of candy; red gives him a towel set; while for a blue light he receives a blanket. When there are fifteen players some one is sure to win, thus making the device a game of chance, pure and simple.

Normally, the game is operated on a percentage basis, which is in favor of the operator. As there are fifteen players, he takes in $1.50 on each play. Thus, for a total of $4.50 taken in on three plays he gives out a box of candy (which costs him about thirty-five cents); a towel set (worth about fifty cents), and a blanket (worth about $2.50).

His total outlay, therefore, is $3.35, with an income of $4.50—a profit of $1.15. By using cheap but flashy prizes the operator makes a fair turnover. He can also run the "Flag Flasher" with less than fifteen players as the percentages are still the same; for if the light stops on an unoccupied bulb, no prize is given out.

The big attractions, however, are the blankets. Every player has his eye on one of them. Therefore the wary operator, who has no scruples about "gaffing" or "doctoring" the game, will sometimes display blankets of exceptional value, and, to

make the game more attractive, will put up larger boxes of candy and better towel sets as prizes. Where, then, is his profit? Obviously, he is due to lose money.

On the contrary, he makes greater profits, for, by a simple process, he "gaffs" the blue lights so that no one can win on them. His problem is this: He must so arrange matters that each blue light can remain lighted when the metal arm stops revolving. The lower explanatory diagram shows how the game is "gaffed," and the problem solved.

The contact posts which control the blue incandescents are sunk a trifle below the others. The metal arm touches each one in passing, so that the bulbs light up. But when the arm is about to stop it will either stop on the post just before one of the blue posts, or, if it slides beyond that post, it will still retain some speed; so much that it will slide over the blue post (lighting the blue bulb for an instant) to the post beyond, where it comes to rest. So, when the operator counts up stock at the end of the evening he finds that his blankets are all there.

A game of this type is not "gaffed" by the manufacturer. The games are turned out to be played fair; any "gaffing" is the work of the operator.

Only a man highly qualified in the psychology of deception could have written this book. Author Walter B. Gibson has had a unique career in subjects bordering on the mysterious. He has written extensively about magic and magicians, and was actually associated with great magicians such as Houdini, Thurston and Blackwell.

From his study of shady devices described in *The Bunco Book*, Walter Gibson drives home the message that "crime does not pay." He created the character of *The Shadow*, whose adventures for years appeared in novel-length form in a magazine bearing the same title, and as a popular weekly radio program that showcased Orson Welles as Lamont Cranston, The Shadow.